Aim higher with *Palgrave Insights in Psychology*

D0802494

From phobias to research methods and relationships to sport psychology, our fantastic range of *Insights* titles take you on a tour of the field, providing a comprehensive, readable introduction to key areas of study within psychology.

Whether you're studying at A-level, university, or have a keen interest that you want to take further, you're sure to find what you need with our *Insights in Psychology* series.

Visit **www.palgrave.com/Insights**
to explore our full range of books.

More titles in this series:

9780230249424   9780230249882   9780230272224   9780230295377

PALGRAVE INSIGHTS IN PSYCHOLOGY
Series Editors: Nigel Holt and Rob Lewis

The Palgrave *Insights in Psychology* series provides short, readable introductions to a wide range of topics across the field of psychology. Accessible and affordable, each book offers clear, up-to-date coverage in a manageable format. Whether you're studying at A-level, university, or have a keen interest that you want to take further, you're sure to find what you need with our *Insights in Psychology* series.

For more information, visit www.palgrave.com/insights

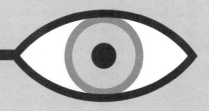

Developmental Psychology

Amanda Ludlow
University of Hertfordshire, UK

and

Roberto Gutierrez
University of Hertfordshire, UK

PALGRAVE INSIGHTS IN PSYCHOLOGY

SERIES EDITORS:
NIGEL HOLT
& ROB LEWIS

palgrave
macmillan

First published 2014 by
PALGRAVE MACMILLAN

Palgrave Macmillan in the UK is an imprint of Macmillan Publishers Limited, registered in England, company number 785998, of Houndmills, Basingstoke, Hampshire RG21 6XS.

Palgrave Macmillan in the US is a division of St Martin's Press LLC, 175 Fifth Avenue, New York, NY 10010.

Palgrave Macmillan is the global academic imprint of the above companies and has companies and representatives throughout the world.

Palgrave® and Macmillan® are registered trademarks in the United States, the United Kingdom, Europe and other countries.

ISBN 978–1–137–32500–6

This book is printed on paper suitable for recycling and made from fully managed and sustained forest sources. Logging, pulping and manufacturing processes are expected to conform to the environmental regulations of the country of origin.

A catalogue record for this book is available from the British Library.

A catalog record for this book is available from the Library of Congress.

Typeset by MPS Limited, Chennai, India.

Printed in China

We would like to dedicate this book to our families,
for all the support over the years.
Thanks!

Contents

List of Figures and Tables

Figures

Tables

Note from Series Editors

We see many hundreds of students every year. When asked what their very favourite part of psychology is, a very large proportion, probably more than half, say 'Child Psychology'. This is perhaps better known as 'Developmental Psychology' and is justifiably one of the most popular aspects of our subject. We begin our journey through the lifespan at our conception and it is here that the authors start the journey for us, but not before a fascinating historical overview of the subject. As experienced teachers, lecturers and authors ourselves, reading through the material in this book has been stimulating and stretching as well as remaining familiar and comfortable. We have not met a good deal of theories here for some years and we both have been spurred on to read further, something we hope you too feel once you have found your way into the book.

Amanda Ludlow is a great talent and an asset to psychology in the United Kingdom. She has published her research into a wide range of developmental disorders, and this book shows that she is more than able to turn her skills to developing teaching and reference materials that students of all abilities will find invaluable. We are delighted that she chose to write with Roberto Gutierrez, also a well-published and extremely exciting psychologist. The book is very accessible and, for its brevity, extremely wide-ranging. The authors have managed to produce a much larger book here than it may seem at first and we are certain it will form a very useful addition to your library.

- *You may be reading this for general interest.* The contents page of this book will give you an idea of the width of coverage the authors have managed to include skilfully. We are certain those with an interest in developmental psychology and childhood on many levels will find material of interest to them here. It is a good starting point, but more than that, it can be read on a number of levels, so we would encourage you to come back to the text for a deeper read once you have completed it. It may well whet your appetite for even more psychology reading.

- *This book may form part of your university reading list.* All psychology degrees include developmental psychology in their delivery. You may well have introductory texts, or larger more specialist detailed books on the subject to read, or this book may be on your reading list. Either way, we encourage you to take a look here. The coverage is both refreshingly couched and will add to your understanding and love of the subject. The glossary is invaluable and it will be extremely useful in developing your thinking, knowledge and in your coursework.

- *You may be using this book while studying for a pre-university course, such as A-level.* It would be a mistake for those responsible for developing pre-university courses to omit developmental psychology, one of the most popular and fascinating areas of the subject, from their specifications and of course they have not. You will find it at General Certificate of Secondary Education (GCSE), A-level and the Baccalaureates as well as in many access courses and other related subjects such as childcare and nursing. This book has been written and edited keeping these courses in mind and we are certain you will find it useful, accessible and engaging.

We recommend this book very strongly to you and are delighted to welcome it to the *Insights in Psychology Series* – an extensive selection of books covering a very wide range of topics in psychology, which has, until now, been missing a vital ingredient – *Developmental Psychology*.

NIGEL HOLT AND ROB LEWIS
Series Editors

Reading Guide

This is one of the books in the *Insights in Psychology* series. There are a range of topics covered in the books, and these have been chosen to carefully reflect the subjects being studied in psychology at a number of levels.

Whether reading for interest, for your degree study or for pre-university courses, such as A-level or other courses where you may find psychology, the material in these books will help you reach the very best of your potential.

The authors of these books have written their books to include material from the specifications of all relevant A-level examination boards in the United Kingdom, these include:

- The Assessment and Qualifications Alliance (AQA)
- The Welsh Joint Education Committee (WJEC)
- Oxford, Cambridge and RSA (OCR)
- EDEXCEL

To keep the qualifications fresh and focussed on the workplace and further education destinations, and to respond to the very latest research and trends in our subject, the examination boards regularly update their curricula. To ensure you have the very latest information we have chosen to include a reading guide online at: www.palgrave.com/insights.

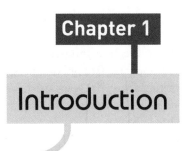

Chapter 1

Introduction

The process in which we develop occurs in continuous stage-like patterns, starting from conception and continuing throughout the lifespan. There are critical developmental milestones that children are expected to reach as their development progresses through from neonatal, infancy, childhood, adolescence, adulthood and older adulthood. The period of child development refers specifically to the changes that occur in biological, social, emotional and cognitive domains from birth to the end of adolescence. By studying which behaviours undergo changes, we can better understand critical time periods in development, possible causes of these changes in behaviours, as well as a better understanding of adulthood.

It is important to note that prior to the 20th century children and their development had been of little interest and had largely been ignored by researchers. Children were not considered complex enough or even capable of making decisions, leading researchers to see little benefit to studying them. However the early 20th century brought with it a new interest in child development and a wave of research has since been carried out with results that continue to show the true value of studying a child's development. The first years of a child's life are now seen as critical for physical, cognitive, social and emotional growth and the foundation for how a child develops in to adulthood. These early years are the building blocks to adult behaviour and will often determine an adult's success or failure in different aspects of his or her life.

👁 Child development in its earliest foundations

During the European Middle Ages, children were not recognised as distinct from adults. When a child turned six or seven years of age and/or was able to live without constant help of a caregiver, she or he belonged to adult society (Aries, 1962). In essence, children were considered miniature adults. However, during the 16th through to 18th century, a new way of looking at childhood emerged. Two philosophers, John Locke and Jean-Jacques Rousseau, writing about 100 years apart, were amongst the first to argue that childhood is an important period that sets the stage for what one becomes later in life.

John Locke (1632–1704) proposed that a child is like a **blank slate (tabula rasa)** and through their interactions with the environment a child will develop his or her unique character and abilities. Locke emphasised the long-term impact of early experience and the responsibility parents bear for forming their children's character. In Locke's view, the environment was seen as the driving force in the child's development. For example, when talking about children's obedience Locke argued that by promoting both obedience *and* curiosity, parents encourage their children to develop into rational attentive people. His views supported the importance of nurture. In contrast, Jean-Jacques Rousseau (1712–1778), the French philosopher and leading proponent of 'natural education', was one of the first to propose that children emerged from the womb with inherent goodness and an **innate set of skills** to begin their own development. Rousseau was a strong opponent of institutions believing them to deplete the individuality and curiosity of a child, but he also wrote of the importance of giving a child the freedom to grow without the intrusion of adults. Rousseau's (1762) philosophy of a liberal education environment rejected the commonly held theory of the time that children were naturally evil and prone to misbehave. He also argued against the need to install authoritarian teachers who ruled the classroom with an iron fist. Instead he believed that greater knowledge was to be gained from children having an active curiosity which would drive them to become independent learners. Rousseau's 1762 novel *Emile* embodied his educational philosophy. Emile is a young boy who is raised completely separate from other children, educated in the outdoors, encouraged to explore his environment. He also recognised the importance of understanding child development, and was one of the first to suggest that children develop in stages (Ornstein, 2012). His views reflect the importance of our innate characteristics, often referred to as 'nature'.

Locke's and Rousseau's opposing views reflect what is still known today as the **nature–nurture debate**. They both were influential in assigning a special status to children and highlighting the importance of early experiences in shaping later development (Martin & Fabes, 2008).

Both Locke's and Rousseau's ideas were founded in philosophy, and it was another philosopher, Dietrich Tiedemann (1748–1803), who pioneered empirical psychology in relation to child development. He kept a journal of observations of his son's sensory, motor, language and cognitive behaviour during the first 30 months of his life. Through **empirical observation**, he hypothesised that children possessed a 'prelinguistic knowledge'.

It was the biologist Charles Darwin who was one of the first to emphasise the developmental nature of infant behaviour. He disputed that children behaviours were created in a fixed and perfect form; instead he suggested that human behaviour evolves slowly. In his book *On the Origins of Species* (1859) he refers to natural selection, a gradual natural process by which more favourable characteristics evolve. He also is responsible for showing common patterns in development of human behaviour and other species (Berman, Rasmussen & Suorni, 1993).

Importantly, Darwin also used the diary method to record observations of children's development. He carefully documented the observations he had gathered during his son's first two years. At the same time, American psychologist Stanley Hall (1844–1924), was also designing new ways in which to study children. Hall was a key figure in the study of children, introducing **questionnaire techniques** and the direct observation of children in psychology as we still consider it today. He was influential in promoting experimental over 'philosophical' methods in psychology.

However it was not until the 1920s that experimental methods in psychology helped psychology to be recognised as a scientific discipline in its own right. It was during this time an American behaviourist, John B. Watson, proposed a theory of behaviouristic principles whereby a child's psychological traits were due in part to the profile of rewards and punishments administered by adults, especially parents. This assumption rested on the belief that children acted in order to maximise pleasure or minimise pain. Therefore actions that bought pleasure would be strengthened and repeated while actions that brought pain would be weakened and discontinued. This view remained popular during the early decades of the 20th century and persisted until the middle of the 20th century. The theory's popularity rested on its ability to explain psychological concepts (such as personality, learning and emotion) in terms of observable behaviours that respond to stimulus. It allowed psychology to be acknowledged for the first time as a natural science.

Summary

- Child development was not considered important until the turn of the 17th century
- John Locke proposed children are born as blank slates (beginning of the 'nature' position)
- Jean-Jacques Rousseau believed children had innate skills which would flourish (beginning of the 'nurture' position)
- Early theories were built around philosophy; Dietrich Tiedemann reported the first empirical observations mapping a child's intelligence and cognitive ability
- Charles Darwin was the first to use diary methods and Stanley Hall was the first to use questionnaires to study child development
- Behaviourism theory moved psychology and the study of children to be seen as a science

◉ Phases in developmental study

Trends in modern theories of child development can be seen to follow political and historical changes or events. We can identify five key historical eras in the study of child development over the last century. The first falls between 1900–1925 and is distinguished by the study of differences, particularly of intellectual ability and personality, among children, motivated largely by the number of immigrant children in the US who were failing school and committing crimes.

The second phase between about 1925–1950 was influenced by Sigmund Freud's psychoanalytic theory. Freud suggested that behaviour is determined by the unconscious mind, a repository of repressed impulses and desires, of which the waking mind is completely unaware, but that determine the way we think, feel and act. According to Freud, all behaviour is motivated by the desire to feel pleasure. That motivation is organised and directed by two instincts: sexuality (Eros) and aggression (Thanatos). In the course of this psychological development, people repress those thoughts or desires that are felt to be uncomfortable or unacceptable to the individual or to society. These contents of the unconscious can cause personality disturbances and even physical symptoms. Although hidden from conscious awareness, these repressed impulses can be deduced from their appearance in dreams or unconscious reactions. A therapist will use techniques such as dream analysis, free association, hypnosis or regression in order to bring the repressed contents of the psyche to the patient's conscious awareness during the long course of the therapy, and in so doing resolve the symptoms they are causing. For the first time physical interventions were challenged by psychological ones.

The third phase was characterised by the **cognitive revolution**, initiated by American linguist Noam Chomsky. His radical view was that children were born with innate ability to use grammar, which they are able to use and then to adapt based on new information they learn through others. Jean Piaget followed on from these ideas, suggesting that children are not passive learners (simply receiving information) but that they are cognitively active in acquiring knowledge through manipulations of objects and ideas.

The fourth phase was defined by British psychiatrist John Bowlby, credited with introducing the concept of infant **attachment**. 'Attachment' was defined as the emotional connection to a person who cares for the infant, created by the infant's pleasure in the presence of the carer and reduction in distress when he or she returns. Attachment is characterised by specific behaviours in children, such as seeking proximity with the attachment figure when upset or threatened (Bowlby, 1969). His early work suggested that the infant and young child should experience 'a warm, intimate, and continuous relationship with his mother (or permanent mother substitute) in which both find satisfaction and enjoyment and that not to do so may have significant and irreversible mental health consequences' (Bowlby, 1951). Both controversial and influential, these views were also used for post-war political purposes to claim *any* separation from the mother was damaging in order to discourage women from working and leaving their children in day care.

The fifth and latest phase is contemporary developmental psychology. Biology has returned to the study of children during the last two decades as a result of recent elegant discoveries in genetics, biology and neuroscience. For example, whilst behavioural studies continually show that language learning develops at a rapid pace during a child's first year of life, neuroimaging techniques have allowed us to see what is happening much earlier by examining both the structural and functional organisation of the brain. Neuroimaging techniques have shown evidence of innate regions in the brain dedicated to speech processing during the first year of life (Dehaene-Lambertz et al., 2006).

Summary

Five key historical eras of child development:

1 Study of individual differences amongst children
2 Psychoanalytic theory
3 Cognitive revolution
4 Attachment theory
5 Biological influence

👁 Themes and stages

Regardless of which theories of child development one supports, or the focus of the domain being looked at, there are key themes that emerge throughout the child development literature. They are:

- Active versus passive child
- Continuity versus discontinuity
- Stability versus change
- Nature versus nurture

Active child versus passive child

It has been heavily debated whether individuals influence their own development through behaviour (active) or whether individuals are at the mercy of their environment (passive). Are infants born as blank slates then altered by experience? Do people who share the same events share the same developmental outcomes? What makes some individuals more active participants in their development than others?

Continuity and discontinuity

Continuity versus discontinuity in development refers to the question of whether development is solely and evenly continuous, or whether it is masked by age-specific periods. Is change sudden or does it happen more gradually? For example, when children start to learn how to speak there is often a sudden language explosion at 18–24 months. However, other skills develop more gradually such as walking.

Continuous development describes development as a relatively smooth process, without sharp or distinct stages through which an individual must pass. In this model, each change in development builds upon previous abilities. In contrast, discontinuous development refers to development as a series of discrete stages, each of which is characterised by at least one task that an individual must accomplish before progressing to the next stage. The notion of a 'stage of development' is central to the discontinuous view of development. A stage of development can be thought of as a particular organisation of a child's knowledge and behaviour that characterises that development at a particular point in time. Factors that promote continuity and discontinuity are stable across the lifespan. Continuous development is thought to be reliant on genetics, physical appearance and environments. In contrast, factors that induce discontinuity can include social roles and life events.

The debate of continuity versus discontinuity is important in addressing whether aspects of one's development relate to later outcomes, with change occurring smoothly through time or progressing through a series of steps that we learn differently at different ages. Implicit in the 'stage theories' of development are ideas of critical periods where particular aspects of development are favoured, for example the difference in language acquisition shown by adults attempting to master a second language compared to young children learning two languages in a bilingual home.

Stability versus change

Is development best characterised by stability? For example, does behaviour such as a child's level of shyness stay relatively stable over time or does it fluctuate? It is often claimed that early experiences influence current and later development. This view then suggests that certain aspects of children's development display stability, in the sense that they are consistent and predictable across time. However research has largely drawn the conclusion that development is characterised by both stability *and* change – for example, personality characteristics such as shyness and the tendency to be aggressive tend to be stable, whilst others such as approach (the tendency to extreme friendliness and lack of caution with strangers) and sluggishness (reacting passively to changing circumstances) are unstable.

Nature versus nurture

The most published theme throughout the child development literature and the one that has generated most controversy is the nature versus nurture debate. This is the question of whether genetic inheritance is the primary influence on a given development track versus the idea that environmental factors (children's experiences, parenting, education, cultural influences and so on) are primarily responsible for development. Today both are recognised as shaping development and the main challenge now is to examine the interplay between the two. This interaction is sometimes referred to as 'epigenesis'. We will continually return to this point throughout the following chapters.

◉ Overview of this book

Numerous theories have been proposed to describe and explain the course of human development, yet over the last hundred or so years, only a few of these theories have stood the test of time. Chapter 2 will consider the most influential developmental theories to date including Freud's psychosexual stage theory, Erikson's psychosocial stage theory, Bandura's social learning theory and Bronfenbrenner's ecological systems theory.

The creation of these theories have stemmed from testable hypotheses about the developing child. Chapter 3 will address the key methods used to study a child's development, from observing the child in a naturalistic setting to manipulating variables in experimental designs. The strengths and limitations to these approaches and the types of research question adopted by these different approaches will be covered. There are also different frameworks in monitoring and assessing these development changes and this chapter will cover the four most common designs: longitudinal, cross-sectional, microgenetic and the time-lag design. Finally, the practicalities and ethical issues associated with researching and safeguarding children will be addressed.

In the subsequent chapters we begin to uncover the key areas of study in developmental psychology, starting with biological development in Chapter 4. Infancy comes with plenty of biological developments, but these changes also continue to occur during early childhood. During these years, a child grows in height and weight while also developing fine motor skills and growing strong muscles. In addition to covering the key biological milestones, we also look at the nature–nurture debate. How much of child's development can be attributed to their genetic inheritance. Here we cover the specific use of twins and adoption in studies designed to uncover the effects of nature and nurture. Identical twins share the exact same genetic code, so some researchers hypothesise that differences between them will show which attributes are influenced by the environment.

Chapter 5 looks at the child's cognitive development covering the three core cognitive theories. Cognitive theory is concerned with the development of a person's thought processes. It also looks at how these thought processes influence how we understand and interact with the world. The foremost cognitive theorist was Jean Piaget, who proposed an idea that seems obvious now, but helped revolutionise how we think about child development: children think differently to adults. Piaget also proposed a theory of cognitive development to account for the steps and sequence of children's intellectual development. Psychologist Lev Vygotsky's theory of socioconstructivism focused on the role of social interaction in cognitive development, and argued that development first takes place socially. He posited that information from the external world is transformed and internalised through language. Since language is both a symbolic system of communication and a cultural tool used to transmit culture and history, it plays an essential part of both language development and a child's understanding of the external world. The premise behind the third cognitive theory discussed in Chapter 5, the information processing account, is that brain function is synonymous with a computer and seeks to explain human learning as the development of networked memory structures.

Chapter 6 focuses on how children develop language, a process starting as soon as a child is born. Whether language is a skill unique to humans has been a question heavily debated. This chapter will cover the research suggesting that features of language might make it unique to humans. The different aspects of language will be introduced alongside evidence suggesting that children develop language in universal stages. The main theories of language development will be discussed, including the empiricist view that language is learnt through observation and reinforcement; the nativist view that language is largely innate and children are born with an ability to learn grammar; and the view that language develops through nature *and* nurture, the interactionist view.

The importance of language in our ability to communicate and socially interact will be apparent from Chapter 6. In Chapter 7 we consider another important skill in our ability to socialise, the way we learn and develop our emotional understanding. The development of our emotions from birth through adolescence will be mapped, providing evidence on how children move from basic primary emotions to those that include more complex skills, such as self-awareness, known as the secondary emotions.

Chapter 8 builds on this topic and addresses how children begin to use their understanding of others' feelings to learn what is right from wrong. The theories of moral development are plentiful, in this chapter we present both those built on reasoning and thought, such as Piaget and Kohlberg's theories of cognitive development, and those built on internal conflicts such as Freud's psychoanalytic theory. Similarities and differences between the theories will be highlighted as well as some of the main criticisms.

Early relationships to caregivers are pivotal to children's later social relationships. In Chapter 9 we explore how children's early attachments with their caregivers impact their development. As children start school and gain independence, it is their relationships with peers that become more important to development. How children make friends and consequences of being a popular versus a neglected child will be discussed. Gender differences in play and social skills is also addressed.

In the final chapter we attempt to bridge the gap between typical development and atypical development. Focusing on the pathways and developmental stages covered in the previous chapters we build on these concepts discussing the development of psychopathology. In addition to covering factors that will enhance the risk of children developing different psychopathologies and how and when the pathway from normal development is thought to diverge, the complex interplay of different causes will be considered. Finally, we describe some of the most common clinical disorders in childhood, illustrating risk factors and also how some of the models of child development introduced in the following chapter account for the development of these conditions.

Chapter 2

Developmental Theories

Children change dramatically in their behaviour throughout their development. However, it is not always clear as to what influences changes in a child's behaviour. For example, is the behaviour of the child affected primarily by the age of the child or do individual factors such as temperament have a larger influence? In order to understand which factors influence these changes in development, psychologists have proposed theories to understand, explain and predict behaviour. Developmental theories help us to organise and make sense of a vast amount of information. They provide a broad and coherent view of the complex influences on human development. These theories also provide a basis for hypothesis development and give a current summary of our knowledge of development.

Several theories have been proposed to describe and explain the course of human development, including children's emotional and social development. Some of the key theories include: Freud's psychosexual stage theory, Erikson's psychosocial stage theory and Bronfenbrenner's ecological systems theory.

In this chapter, we will examine:
- The importance of developmental theories and their key features
- Who the key theorists are and what similarities and differences exists between their theories
- How developmental theories have changed since they were first introduced

◉ What makes a good developmental theory?

There are several important features that are integral to all theories of development. As Miller (1993) proposed, any good developmental theory needs to focus on changes over time in behaviour in the particular domain of functioning. Taking the language domain as an example – how does a child go from speaking one or two words to a rapidly expanding repertoire of vocabulary? As well as describing the changes a good theory also needs to be able to explain how these changes take place. Moreover, good theories should be testable, refutable, modifiable and reliable.

Some of the key development theories are:

- Psychodynamic theory
- Psychosocial theory
- Behaviourism and social learning theory (learning theories)
- Ethological theory
- The bioecological model of development
- Life course theory
- Cognitive development theories

We will now discuss in depth each of these theories.

◉ Psychodynamic theory

The key feature of the psychodynamic approach is a focus on trying to 'get inside the head' of individuals in order to understand how their life experiences have impacted on their behaviour. This can include trying to understand how the individual makes sense of close relationships, what they experience and, importantly, how they actually perceive their world. The psychodynamic approach, most commonly linked with children and adults undergoing some form of counselling, is an approach that is still used in various aspects of everyday psychology. Theories falling under the heading of the psychodynamic approach all see human functioning as based upon the interaction of drives and forces within the person and between the different structures of their personality.

Whilst the layperson is probably most familiar with the founder of the psychodynamic approach, Sigmund Freud, there are many other theorists such as Jung (1963), Adler (1927) and Erikson (1950) who have expanded upon the work of Freud.

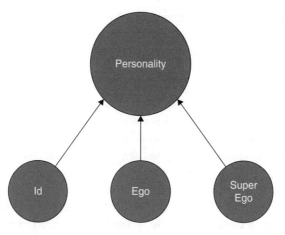

Figure 2.1 Psychodynamic theory: key principles

Basic assumptions in the psychodynamic approach include:

- Unconscious motives can powerfully control our behaviour and feelings
- Childhood experiences are the root cause of how we develop as adults. They are thought to have a direct effect on both behaviour and feelings as adults including any psychological problems
- All behaviour is intentional, even if it is only at the unconscious level
- Personality is made up of three parts: the id, the ego and the superego
- Behaviour is motivated by two instinctual drives stemming from the id: Eros (the sex drive and the life instinct) and Thanatos (the aggressive drive and the death instinct)
- The unconscious mind (the id and superego) can be in constant conflict with the conscious mind (the ego)
- Our instinctual drives are modified by different conflicts at different times in childhood that then shape our personality

Sigmund Freud 1856–1939

Freud coined the term 'psychodynamic' to describe the constant conflict between opposing forces within the 'psyche' or internal world. This internal personality state was considered to have three distinct elements or structures (id, ego and superego) otherwise known as 'it', 'me' and 'above me' respectively. The theory is sometimes also referred to as the structural model. Freud also described 'instincts' or 'drives' that were seen as innate, universal and constantly felt, such as pleasure and guilt. Freud's theory was mainly concerned with the management of conflicts between these drives, with individuals attempting to maximise gratification whilst minimising guilt and punishment.

The id consists of all the inherited personality, including the sex life (Eros which contains the libido) and aggressive (death) instinct. The id is the impulsive and unconscious part of the psyche and responds directly by instinct. It is present at birth and involves an unconscious impulse toward fulfilment of needs. The id demands immediate satisfaction and works on the **'pleasure principle'** (Freud, 1920), satisfaction of needs brings pleasure and when denied we experience displeasure which we (consciously or unconsciously) seek to avoid.

The ego is the part of the id which develops next in order to mediate between the unrealistic id and the reality of an external world where immediate gratification may not be possible (Freud, 1923).The role of ego is to delay desires for instant gratification and redirects it in to more realistic and appropriate ways to meet one's needs. The ego works according to the **'reality principle'**, finding the most realistic ways to satisfying the id's demands without causing harm to itself or the id (McLeod, 2008).

The superego develops around four or five years of age and represents the incorporation of the values and morals of society. The superego's function is to control the id's impulses, especially those which society condemns, sex and aggression. It provides the individual with the standards by which to regulate one's moral conduct and take pride in one's accomplishments. The superego consists of two systems: the conscience and the 'ideal self'. The conscience punishes the ego through causing feelings of guilt. The ideal self is the internal construct of how you ought to be, how you should treat people and what you should want to do. It aims for perfection. If behaviour falls short of the ideal self, then guilt occurs; when we achieve how we ought to behave the superego feels proud. The two systems are largely determined by our parents' values, their guidance and how we are brought up.

The superego's demands often work in opposition to the id's. The ego attempts to resolve conflicts between the opposing demands. Unresolved conflicts between the id-ego and superego can lead to a **fixation** or blockage in development. Consequences on behaviour can result in excessive dependence or a personality built around manipulation.

Freud also emphasised the particular importance of the first five years of one's childhood for adult functioning. He believed the early years were dominated by a psychosocial conflict surrounding sexual drive. This led Freud to evolve a model of human development built on psychosexual stages. Sexual development has two main phases: the pre-genital phase comprising of oral, anal and phallic stages, occurring from birth to about age six, followed by a period called latency. Then a second phase, called the genital stage, begins with puberty and determines the final outcome of mature sexual life.

Each stage is known by the area of the body directly associated with the erogenous zone at the centre of a conflict between instinctual drive and societal demands: oral, anal and phallic. Each of these zones is associated with a vital somatic (or 'bodily') function; the oral zone with feeding, the anal zone with defecation and the phallic zone with sexual gratification. It is through the pleasurable sensations that accompany fulfilment of any of these somatic functions that an erogenous zone becomes established. A need to repeat this pleasurable sensation arises, which then becomes separate from the somatic function.

Whilst most individuals will pass through each stage smoothly, problems arise when too little or too much gratification at any stage results in an individual becoming fixated. The precise impact on development varies depending on what stage the frustration or indulgence happened and what form it took.

The first of the psychosexual stages is the **oral stage** where the mouth of the infant is the primary erogenous zone. It forms the basis of an infant's first human relationship – biological (nutritive) and psychological (emotional) – and lasts until around 18 months of age. If a child is weaned either before or after he or she is developmentally ready, he or she might develop a maladaptive oral fixation leading to a failure to resolve emotional conflicts of this stage. An infantile oral fixation (sucking) would develop into an obsession with oral stimulation. This type of personality has a stronger tendency to smoke, drink alcohol, over eat or bite his or her nails. Beyond weaning, an oral fixation could occur when a child is neglected and insufficiently fed or when overprotected and over fed. An oral fixation could have two effects. A neglected child may become psychologically dependent adult, gullible and a perpetual follower, whereas an overly protected child may develop pessimism and aggression toward others (Millon, Millon, Meagher, Grossman & Ramanath, 2004).

The **anal stage** is thought to occur from 18 months to 3 years old. The child's pleasure surrounds eliminating and retaining faeces. The child has to learn to control anal stimulation. In terms of its effects on personality, anal fixation can result in an obsession with cleanliness, perfection and control (anal retentive personality). It may also result in the polar opposite behaviour and the person becomes messy and disorganised (anal expulsive personality).

Around three to six years old the **phallic stage** takes place. The pleasure zones switch from the mouth to the genitals. Freud's account of this stage focussed on what happens to boys only. Freud referred to boys' unconscious sexual desires for their mother leading to rivalry with the father as they compete for their mother's affections. Boys are thought to develop a fear of their father castrating them due to these feelings. This group of feelings is known as the Oedipus complex (after the Greek mythological figure who accidently killed his father and married his mother). Freud believed that boys will eventually decide to identify with their father rather than fight him. By identifying with his father, the boy acknowledges his own masculinity and suppresses the feelings for the mother. The Electra complex (named after another Greek character) is a term coined later psychologists to refer to females going through a similar stage and developing feelings for their father. However the Electra complex was heavily refuted by Freud. According to psychoanalysts, a fixation at this stage could result in sexual deviances (both overindulgence and avoidance) and confused sexual identity (Stevenson-Snell, 1996).

The **latency period** ranges from six to puberty and is thought to focus on the child's need to interact and play mostly with same sex peers. The final stage is defined by puberty onwards and called the **genital stage**. Puberty is thought to awaken sexual urges. Adolescents direct their urges to partners of the opposite sex, with the primary focus on pleasure being the genitals.

Evaluation of the theory

There have been many criticisms of Freud's theory, with a large proportion of the critics focusing on the methods used to interpret data. For example, the interpretation of the data on which the theory is built tends to be heavily reliant on subjective measures (explanations of dreams) rather than any objective measure. This means that interpreters are able to favour claims that support their beliefs, ignoring those that don't. The theoretical constructs, including the idea that behaviour is determined by the unconscious mind, mean that their existence is virtually impossible to either validate or dispute. It is the lack of empirical data available to support the theory that has led opponents to challenge the idea that the psychodynamic approach should even be considered a science (Fowler, 2010). Freud also mostly dealt with adults in both his research and clinical practice. However, supporters of psychodynamic theory instead choose to highlight the virtues of the theory, including being able to account for the complexity and irrationality of human behaviour and also the considerable number of people who have been treated using psychoanalytical therapy (Mace, Moorey & Roberts, 2013). In addition, the theory takes a case approach and rather than seeing all people as the same, considers crucial early individual differences impacting upon development. Importantly the theory has two main strengths, the ideas that childhood experiences can shape your adult personality and also that not all behaviour occurs at the conscious level (Hoffman, 2010).

Summary

- Emphasis is on the belief that forces or dynamics within the individual are responsible for his or her behaviour.
- Modern theories emphasise the role of unconscious processes in our behaviour, but put less emphasis on sexual and aggressive instincts.
- Personality is made up of three structures:
  - id (pleasure principle)
  - ego (conflict with reality, ego emerges)
  - superego (internalise parental and society values).
- Five stages – oral, anal, phallic, latency and genital stages (each named after an erogenous zone).

◉ Psychosocial theory (Erik Erikson 1902–1990)

Erikson's theory combined both internal psychological factors and external social factors. He believed that there were eight stages of

							Integrity versus Despair
						Generativity versus Stagnation	
					Intimacy versus Isolation		
				Identity versus Identity Diffusion			
			Industry versus Inferiority				
		Initiative versus Guilt					
	Autonomy versus Shame						
Trust versus Mistrust							
Birth to 1 year	1 to 3 years	3 to 6 years	6 years to adolescence	Adolescence (10–20 years)	Young Adulthood (20–40 years)	Middle Adulthood (40–60 years)	Old age (60 +years)

Figure 2.2 Erikson's stages of development

development from birth until adulthood. Each stage appeared in a set order and built upon the other. Each stage focused on a specific challenge (or crisis) that needed to be resolved during that stage in order to move effectively onto the next stage of development. Failure to resolve the crisis in early stages may continue to affect the child's later development.

The resolution of each crisis was thought to depend on not only the individual child's characteristics but also the support provided by the social environment.

1 *Learning basic trust versus mistrust.* This stage develops within the first two years of life. The child, well handled, nurtured and loved, is able to develop a good level of trust. A child mistreated will become insecure and distrustful.

2 *Learning autonomy versus shame.* The second stage occurs with early childhood and is linked to behaviour often associated with the

'terrible twos'. Children show tantrums, stubbornness and negativism. A 'well-parented' child will emerge from this stage with clear sense of independence without shameful behaviour as they have learnt to negotiate with parents what they can and cannot do.

3 *Learning initiative versus guilt.* The third stage develops at the play age or later preschool years. A healthy child will learn to broaden play skills including fantasy, to co-operate with others, to lead as well as follow. In contrast, an unhealthy child is prevented from joining in due to guilt and fear. He or she is often on the periphery of the group, unable to engage in fantasy play and heavily dependent on adults.

4 *Industry versus inferiority.* The fourth stage occurs in primary school years. Here the child learns to master more formal life skills including relating to peers through rules, play becomes more rule based and more team based. The child achieves mastery of social skills, reading and arithmetic and develops more self-discipline. The child who has successfully mastered their way through earlier stages will be full of trust and will have the necessary skills such as trust and autonomy to be able to learn easily enough to be industrious. The mistrusting child will often experience defeat and inferiority.

5 *Learning identity versus identity diffusion.* This stage is thought to occur from early adolescence up and until early adulthood. An identity crisis of some form usually occurs in all boys and girls. Here minor delinquency is experimented with, children often rebel and self-doubt is present. Adolescence is a time when self-certainty develops providing the person with the assurance to strive for what he or she wants and anticipates achievement rather than to be controlled by fear. A successful adult will seek out leadership and will develop a set of ideals that are socially congruent and desirable.

6 *Learning intimacy versus isolation.* True intimacy is experienced for the first time with serious relationships and long-standing friendships characteristic of this stage.

7 *Learning generativity versus self-absorption.* In adulthood, generativity is the ability to become productive in society and to set an example for future generations. In this stage the interest in parenthood also appears.

8 *Learning integrity versus despair.* In the final stage and as long as the seven stages have all been successfully resolved, the adult will easily be able to develop integrity. They will be independent, able to trust, have a clearly defined role in life and developed a self-concept that they are happy with. They can be intimate and proud of all that they create. If one or more of the earlier psychosocial roles have not been resolved, the person may view himself and his life with despair.

Whilst being insightful and plausible, these eight stages of Erikson's theory remain solely as descriptions. No evidence exists to show that all children or adults pass through eight stages neither that failure to resolve earlier stages will have repercussions for the child's development.

Evaluation of theory

Compared to Freud, Erikson worked mainly with children and adolescents, so his ideas were derived from directly relevant experience. One of the biggest strengths of his theory was not only the inclusion of eight successive stages, but that each stage met with an inherent crisis. Rather using the term 'crisis' in the catastrophic sense, Erikson chose this term to represent a turning point or a sensitive period in the child's life that could lead to both successful and unsuccessful outcomes (Hoare, 2002). He also emphasised the importance of a range of sociocultural factors and not just sexuality. Some critics of his theory have argued that identity formation occurs throughout adulthood and is not 'fixed' by adolescence as implied by Erikson. Similar to criticism of Freud, the approach has been also been criticised for lacking research to support and validate its theories.

Summary

- Emphasises the role of social and cultural factors and proposes the idea that development continues throughout the life course.
- Erikson's (1963) underlying basis for human development is an interaction of three different systems: the somatic system, the ego system and the societal system.

The contribution of Freud and Erikson

There are some important similarities between Erikson and Freud that are still influential on contemporary development psychology. Both theories are created around the assumption that the experiences of the early years will impact on our later behaviours. Both Freud's instinctive id and Erikson's Trust versus Mistrust stage highlight the importance of early attachment behaviour in fulfilling our basic needs. They also propose the 'healthy' development of ego, the ability to have autonomy whilst meeting the demands of our social encounters as well as the need to be independent whilst also having an active social engagement with peers and families. The development of the superego has been proposed by both theorists to be a crucial developmental milestone that takes place through transmission of family and community values and moral integration. Finally, they both emphasised the effect unconscious thoughts can play on the emotional development of children into adults (Jenvey, 2013). However, a key limitation of both theories is the absence of any examination of the influence of culture on how a child is parented, or its effect on a child's early development. Both theories were also criticised for the suggestion that sex differences occur due to biological influences. Importantly, modern neuropsychological studies have shown support for this suggestion, with sex differences being found in a vast array of different behaviours (e.g. play, aggression, learning & cognition) (Hines, 2006).

◉ Behavioural theories (learning theories)

Learning theories, in contrast to most developmental theories, are not generally stage based. Behaviour is not considered fixed at certain stages and are not explicitly linked to the different ages of the child. Instead the principles that govern behaviour are thought to be accurate at every age. The focus is on the basic relationship between the stimulus and the response, investigating situations that cause responses to occur most predictably.

John B. Watson (1913) coined the term 'behaviourism'. This theory assumes that behaviour is observable and can be correlated with other observable events. Behaviourism's goal is to explain relationships between antecedent conditions (stimuli), behaviour (responses) and consequences (rewards and punishment).

The core concepts of behaviourism are:

- *The 'blank slate'.* Children enter the world as a 'blank slate' but have a capacity to learn. What is learned depends on the environment surrounding the child.

- *The behavioural focus.* In opposition to Freud's dependence on unobservable concepts (the existence of the 'id', etc.) study is focused only on observable behaviour, aiming to discover the environmental stimuli that produce it.
- *Environmentalist determinism.* Like Freud, Watson believes that an individual's behaviour is not produced by 'free will' but entirely dependent on their experience. In this model, experience of their environment.
- *Conditioning.* The main process through which we learn is 'conditioning'. The concepts of 'learning' and 'conditioning' are closely associated.

Ivan Pavlov (1849–1936) in the late 19th century was the first to propose **classical conditioning** as stimulus–response learning. Whilst experimenting with dogs, Pavlov noticed that dogs would start salivating when it was time to be fed. Pavlov's dogs, restrained in an experimental chamber, were presented with meat powder and they had their saliva surgically collected. The dogs were found to salivate before the meat was presented, whether by the presence of the handler or the clicking noise of the meat dispenser. Pavlov investigated this further by pairing the meat with various other stimuli such as a bell ringing. After the meat powder and bell (auditory stimulus) were presented together several times, the bell was presented alone. Pavlov's dogs responded by salivating to the sound of the bell, even without food being present, a response called a 'conditioned response'.

In these experiments, the meat powder is considered an unconditional stimulus (UCS) and the dog's salivation the unconditioned response (UCR). The bell is neutral stimulus until after repeating pairings of the bell with food the dog *learns* to associate the bell with food. Then the bell becomes a conditioned stimulus (CS) and produces the conditioned response (CR) of salivation. The concepts can be present in a diagrammatic form, as below.

$$\text{meat powder} = \text{salivation}$$
$$\text{(UCS)} \qquad \text{(UCR)}$$

$$\text{meat powder} + \text{bell} = \text{salivation}$$
$$\text{(UCS)} \qquad \text{(NS)} \qquad \text{(UCR)}$$

$$\text{bell} = \text{salivation}$$
$$\text{(CR)} \quad \text{(UCR)}$$

Pavlov demonstrated how stimulus–response bonds are formed, which many consider the building blocks of understanding children's learning.

Watson extended Pavlov's work by applying it to human beings. In 1921, Watson studied an 11-month-old infant child, Albert. The goal of the study was to condition Albert to become afraid of a white rat by associating the rat with a very loud, jarring noise (UCS). At first Albert showed no sign of fear when he was presented with a rat, but once the rat was repeatedly paired with the loud noise (UCS), Albert developed a fear of rats. Ten days after conditioning ended his fear of the rat was much less marked. This dying out of a learned response is called 'extinction'. However even a full month after conditioning ended some fear was still evident. Watson's findings suggested that classical conditioning could cause some phobias in humans.

$$\text{Jarring Noise} + \text{Rat}$$
$$\text{(UCS)} \quad \text{(NS)}$$

$$\text{Jarring Noise} = \text{Fear of Rat}$$
$$\text{(CS)} \quad \text{(UCR)}$$

Operant conditioning was first introduced by B.F. Skinner. Operant conditioning (sometimes referred to as 'instrumental conditioning') is a method of learning that occurs through rewards and punishments for behaviour. Through operant conditioning, an association is made between a given behaviour and a consequence for that behaviour. In operant conditioning, any event that strengthens or increases the chances of the behaviour occurring is called 'reinforcement'. 'Positive reinforcement' is a response strengthened by the addition of something, such as praise or a direct reward. An example would be a child being given a sticker on completion of tidying their room. 'Negative reinforcement' is a response strengthened by the removal of something considered unpleasant, for example, the child being told they will not have to tidy their room if they have been good all day. In both cases of reinforcement the behaviour increases. As well as reinforcement,

	Reinforcement increase behaviour	Punishment decrease behaviour
Positive stimulus: Something added	Positive reinforcement Add something to increase behaviour	Positive punishment Add something to decrease behaviour
Negative stimulus: Something removed	Negative reinforcement Remove something to increase behaviour	Negative punishment Remove something to decrease behaviour

Table 2.1 The effect of positive and negative reinforcement on children's behaviour

operant conditioning can include punishment. 'Positive punishment' involves the presentation of an unfavourable event or outcome in order to weaken the response that follows. 'Negative punishment' occurs when a favourable event or outcome is removed after the behaviour occurs. Table 2.1 shows how these concepts work to strengthen or weaken behaviours.

Social modelling or social learning theory (Bandura, 1977) is the behavioural proposal that people learn from one another, via observation, imitation and modelling. The theory suggests that learning occurs through observation of consequences. A person does not have to personally understand and learn what behaviours are appropriate for that setting. Bandura's social learning theory can be demonstrated with the Bobo doll experiment. In the early 1960s Albert Bandura studied children's behaviour after watching an adult model act aggressively towards a Bobo doll (an inflatable toy designed to fall down immediately if hit but then immediately spring back up). There have been many variations of experiments using the Bobo doll. In his 1961 experiment (Bandura, Ross & Ross, 1961), 36 boys and 36 girls aged 37–69 months took part. Of the72 children, 24 were exposed to an aggressive model and 24 to a non-aggressive model, the remaining 24 children were controls. Groups were divided into males and females to ensure half were exposed to models of the same sex and the other half to models of the opposite sex.

There were two parts to the experiment. In the first stage each child was individually bought into a playroom with an adult model. The children sat in one corner of the room with lots of desirable children's toys. The adult model was seated in another corner containing a toy set, a mallet and an inflatable Bobo doll. During the aggressive model scenario, the adult showed aggression to toward the Bobo doll, including hitting and punching the face with hand and the mallet and would verbally assault the doll: 'Kick him', 'Hit him'. After 10 minutes the adult and the child left the playroom. In the non-aggressive scenario, the adult played with all the other toys for 10 minutes ignoring the Bobo doll. In the control group there was no adult model.

In the next stage the children were taken to a second room and allowed to play with toys. The children were stopped after 10 minutes and in order to build up frustration were told they were no longer allowed to play with the toys. The children then went back to the original room and were allowed to play toys of their choice for 20 minutes. The experimenter measured the the number of times the children showed physical aggression (punching, kicking, hitting with the mallet), verbal aggression and any aggression not imitating the adult model. Those children who participated in the aggressive adult modelling scenario were more likely to act aggressively themselves. Boys showed more aggressive play than girls, and both showed more aggressive play when observing the same sex model. The experimenters concluded from the study that children observing adult behaviour are influenced to think that this type of behaviour is acceptable.

Amongst the criticisms of the study are that it was unethical and morally wrong, as the participants were manipulated to respond in an aggressive way (Wortman, Loftus & Weaver, 1999); that the children might have imitated models as they interpreted the model's actions to be instructions and therefore not reflective of how they would behave in real life; and that no history of the children taking part in the study is available, so it is unclear if any of children were previously exposed to aggression at home. In addition, the social learning theory more generally has been criticised for failing to acknowledge the biological make-up of the children, for example their individual brain development or learning differences as an aspect of development (Isom, 1998).

Evaluation of behavioural theories

The methods used to study behaviourism have largely been praised for their empirical approach and attempts to demonstrate both cause and effect. However an important criticism of behaviourism is that it neglects the thinking processes. The theory also fails to explain why some behaviour occurs even in the absence of being conditioned. In contrast the strength of social learning theory is that considers cognitive factors, such as the thought processes involved, which mediate between stimuli and responses. For example, if a child previously had negative interactions with others they will be more likely to develop a hostile attribution bias (tendency to see others intent as hostile) and are more likely to act aggressively (Bradshaw, Goldweber & Garbarino, 2013).

Critics of the social learning theory believe the research can often be conducted in rather an artificial setting. For example, it has been argued that the children in Bandura's studies may have intentionally produced the behaviour they thought was expected of them. It is difficult to determine whether the children's behaviour could be generalised to different settings such as a home or school environment. Social learning theories are also criticised for the amount of weight they give to environmental factors influencing behaviour while ignoring other aspects such as genetic predisposition or sex-based neurological differences, for example.

Summary

- *Behaviourism* – Children can be moulded in the direction desired if adults carefully control stimulus–response associations (Watson).
- *Skinner's operant conditioning* – The likelihood of a child's behaviour recurring can be controlled with reinforcement and punishment.
- *Bandura's social learning theory* – Also supported principles of conditioning and reinforcement but explained how children acquire these responses.

The influence of environment on development: three theories

Ethological theory

Ethological theory is built around the idea that the natural environment has an effect on development. From the ethological perspective, the selective pressures of the environment, not the individual's genetic makeup, are responsible for changes in behaviour. Ethology stresses that behaviour is strongly influenced by biology and is tied to evolution and characterised by critical or sensitive periods. Within this framework, the transmission of behaviours and traits through genetics plays a significant role in the development of even complex behaviours such as emotion and thinking.

Some of the foundations of ethological theory have stemmed from Charles Darwin's work on natural selection. Individuals in a species show a wide range of variation, due to differences in genes. Individuals with characteristics most suited to the environment are more likely to survive and reproduce. The genes that allowed the individuals to be successful are therefore passed to the offspring in the next generation. Individuals that are poorly adapted to their environment are less likely to survive and reproduce. This means that their genes are less likely to be passed to the next generation.

The origins of the ethological perspective in psychology are founded in work looking at (non-human) animals. Based on careful observation of animals in their natural habitat (as opposed to a laboratory environment as in behaviourism), researchers such as Nikolaas Tinbergen and Konrad Lorenz noted that many animal species are equipped with a number of behavioural patterns that promote their survival (Burkhardt, 2005). For example, Lorenz (1937) studied what he called 'imprinting' (following behaviour) in goslings. Imprinting is a behaviour which is acquired extremely rapidly when the chick hatches and serves to ensure that the offspring will stay close to their mother so as to be fed and protected from predators. In birds such as geese, imprinting occurs during a restricted time period of development known as a 'critical period'. Baby geese (and ducklings) are born prepared to develop attachment and will imprint upon the first things they see whether it be their mother, a substitute of their mother, such as Lorenz himself, or even a pull-toy. This illustrates the importance of a critical period, a fixed time period very early in development during which certain behaviours optimally emerge. It also highlights that a tendency to acquire a particular behaviour is 'pre-programmed' but the support of the environment is critical to actual acquisition of the behaviour.

Whilst imprinting behaviours are not thought to occur in humans, the concept of a critical period has been looked at in the context of child development. Bornstein (1989) suggests the term 'sensitive period' as a better term for humans. This concept will be returned to throughout the book (particularly Chapters 6 and 7 when we address language development and attachment).

One of the ethologists' most useful tools is the ethogram, a detailed description of an observed subject's behaviours in a natural or uncontrived a setting as possible. Each behaviour action is precisely defined so that ethograms can be used as reliable and comparable data sources. Researchers have used similar techniques in the study of child development. In particular, much of the work of John Bowlby addressing child attachment behaviour not only focused on the idea of pre-programmed behaviours needed for survival but also adopted observation studies influenced by the work of ethologists Tinbergen, Lorenz and Robert Hinde.

Ethological theory provides a good explanation of biological and evolutionary development and counters criticism of behaviourism by putting an emphasis on observing behaviour in a natural or normal setting. However, critics of the theory would argue that the critical and sensitive periods are too rigid. There is no evidence of an absolute critical or sensitive period, rather, there is a principle of relative time effects (Ramey & Ramey, 1998)

The bioecological model

The **bioecological model** (Bronfenbrenner, 1974) focuses on an individual's development with greater emphasis placed on the role of his/her social contexts. Development occurs in a set of overlapping ecological systems. All of these systems operate together to influence what a person becomes as he/she develops. In Urie Bronfenbrenner's model, the individual is at the centre of the system. There are several ecological systems:

- *Microsystem*– The immediate social settings (family, school, work, church, peer group) in which an individual is involved. This system is focused on the face-to-face interaction with others.
- *Mesosystem*– This system links two microsystems together, directly or indirectly (e.g., parent–teacher conference, overtime at work).
- *Exosystem*– Settings in which the person does not actively participate but in which significant decisions are made, affecting the individuals who do interact directly with the person (e.g., neighbourhood/community structures that affect the functioning of smaller systems, such as newspapers or television).
- *Macrosystem*– The blueprints for defining and organising the institutional life of the society, including overarching patterns of culture, politics or economy.

In a later review of his bioecological theory, Bronfenbrenner also included in his model the notion that development occurs in historical time (the 'chronosystem') (Bronfenbrenner & Morris, 1998). The chronosystem involves all aspects of time from historical events such as recession to the timing of individual events, such as the onset of puberty and how they impact development.

Whilst the ecological theory shows a systematic examination of both macro and micro dimensions of environmental systems, the theory was initially criticised for failing to consider important biological factors, a problem addressed by Bronfenbrenner in further revisions of his model which places greater emphasis on the role of the biological person.

Life course theory

Another theory emphasising the importance of time in development is the life course theory (Elder Jr, 1995; Elder, 1998). There are four key concepts to this theory:

1 *Human lives are situated in historical time and place.* The time of birth will determine the developmental trajectory of the child. This can happen through the cohort effect where people from different birth cohorts are affected by different events. This can also happen through a period effect, where a historical event exerts a relatively uniform effect across different birth cohorts.

2 *Developmental studies must pay attention to the time of our lives.* Social roles and events define norms for behaviour at different ages. Consider a woman who becomes pregnant as a teenager, compared to a woman who has children later in life. The same life event occurring at different stages in the life course will have considerably different impacts on each of the women's developmental pathways.

3 *Human lives are interdependent or linked with each other.* Our lives are built around our relationships with people (family, peer and romantic relationships). For example the early attachments we form with our parents are likely to impact the attachments we form with our children.

4 *Human beings have the ability to make decisions and power to change their lives.* How we choose to behave with and relate to other people

serves to shape and select the environment that we actually experience. Planning one's decisions can act as a protective factor, whereas lack of planning can be a risk factor with poorer outcomes.

Similar to Brofenbrenner's bioecological theory, emphasis is placed on the environment shaping development. However, whilst Bronfenbrenner places the individual at the centre of the model of development, Elder's view was that social environments should be the major emphasis of developmental studies.

Summary of theories

- *The ethological perspective.* An emphasis on observations of behaviour in normal contexts. Key developmental concepts are 'imprinting' and the 'critical period'.
- *The bioecological model* (Bronfenbrenner, 1979). The individual is at the centre of a system which includes four layers. Each layer can impact development.
- *Life course theory* (Elder, 1995, 1998).Emphasises the role of time as a developmental context.

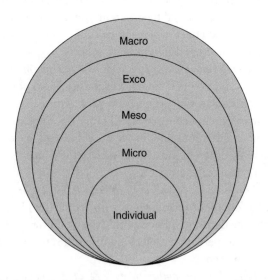

Figure 2.3 Brofenbrenner's model
Source: Adapted from Keenan (2006).

⊙ Three cognitive development theories

Cognitive development refers to a child's development or construction of a mental model of the world. In contrast to psychoanalytical theories stressing the importance of their unconscious thoughts, cognitive theories emphasise their conscious thoughts. There are three important cognitive theories:

1 Piaget's cognitive development theory (Piaget, 1983)
2 Vygotsky's sociocultural theory development (Vygotsky, 1978, 1986)
3 The information processing approach (Siegler, 1996).

These are only briefly summarised below as we return to these theories in Chapter 5 in much more detail.

Jean Piaget (1896–1980)

- A child is an active participant in creating their own understanding of the world.
- Our cognitive structures (minds) are adaptations which help ensure that our knowledge provides a good 'fit' to the world.
- Cognitive development is a process of revision (equilibrium).
- There are four stages: sensorimotor (birth to two years); preoperational (two to seven years); concrete operational (seven to twelve years); formal operational (from twelve years).

Lev Vygotsky (1896–1934)

- Also believed children are active learners
- Emphasised social interaction
- Believed children acquire knowledge and skills through social interactions with more experienced and more knowledgeable members of society
- Described two levels (interpersonal/intrapersonal)

Information processing

- Based on the analogy between the digital computer and human mind

- Helps map out the series of steps describing the flow of information through the human mind
- Adds precision, readily testable, identifiable mechanisms which underlie development

The main criticism often levelled at cognitive theories is the idea that our thoughts and our memories solely construct how we see the world. Whilst Vygotsky's theory highlights the importance of social factors, cognitive theories are generally criticised for ignoring both the important biological and social influences on a child's development.

Chapter 3

Research Methodology

We can understand what influences behavioural and mental processes by using the scientific method of acquiring knowledge through observation and/or experimentation. Observation helps researchers answer the question 'What is really happening?' and its product is descriptive research. Experimentation can help the researcher answer 'Why might this be happening?' and its product is explanatory research. Good accurate descriptive research can challenge prevailing assumptions about how something is and provoke questions leading to the formation of new explanations derived from well-designed experiments. There are five basic steps to carrying out explanatory research: (1) identify the problem; (2) generate a hypothesis – a testable explanation of some phenomenon; (3) test the hypothesis by collecting data; (4) analyse the collected data; (5) make a decision on whether the data supports or refutes the hypothesis. These basic steps remain true for both research on adult and child populations. However, infants and children can be more difficult to test than some adults and they are also more vulnerable than adults. Therefore some research methods are seen as more appropriate for research on child development.

In this chapter, we will examine:
- Different data gathering methods
- Experimental versus correlational designs
- Group assignment methods
- Sampling methods
- Ethical considerations when working with children

When describing research in development the variables that are being explored as an influence on the behaviour outcome are referred to as independent variables (IV) and the outcome is referred to as the dependent variable (DV). For example, when looking at gender difference in children's aggressive play, 'gender' would be the IV and the number of aggressive behaviour shows (or some other measured observation) would be the DV.

Since children's behaviour emerges over time, age is often a particularly important variable in research. This means that some outcomes are a result of growing older and gradually change as time passes. However there are also many other issues and questions in development that are not age related. These can include variables such as socioeconomic status (SES), level of education, religion, gender, drug use, etc. Child development researchers are interested in all of the variables (independent variable) that influence the outcome of the person (dependent variable)

Research methods

Amongst the most common research methods in development research are those using observation techniques to collect data.

Naturalistic observation

This involves studying the behaviour of children in their natural environment without any attempt to intervene. For example, in order to understand how children socialise with their peers, a researcher might decide to observe their behaviour at school during playtime. The situation is not manipulated by the investigator neither has the situation been created. There are many advantages to carrying out naturalistic observations. The key one is that it allows observation of behaviour exactly as it occurs in the real world and therefore retains an element of ecological validity. It helps to establish the external validity of research findings. If you see the behaviour occurring in real life, you can be more confident that what you learn from your sample can be extended to others outside your sample.

One problem with observation studies is reactivity, when subjects who know they are being observed will often alter their behaviour. For example, when children are aware that aggressive play may be socially unacceptable, the presence of an unknown adult observer in the playground may inhibit such behaviour resulting in a distortion of the data even if they are unaware of the reason for the observer's presence. Removing the unnatural element may be possible by recruiting observers from the normal environment (such as a parent-observer, or teaching staff at a school).

There are several ways that researchers can reduce the chances of reactivity. (1) Unobtrusive observation is when people are unaware that they are being observed. (2) Deception would involve not telling participants the real reason that they are being observed and leaving them blind to their role in the study. These two both ensure that those being watched react naturally. (3) One step further is that both the subject and the experimenter are blind as to the true role of the subject. This is referred to as a double-blind study. However there are ethical implications to both watching people without their permission and deceiving participants and we will cover this later in the chapter.

Structured observation

This is where the researcher sets up a situation where they might be able to see the behaviour that they are interested in observing. It is seen as observation with intervention, because the behaviour would not have occurred at that time and place had the experimenter not created the situation. Whilst the naturalistic observation involves passive observation, and a field experiment actively manipulating the conditions, structured observations provide a middle ground between the two. For example a structured observation method may be chosen to observe the effect of delayed language development on the social skills of children. A set of social tasks may be set up to observe the child's reaction in them. Significant weaknesses of structured observation include the variability in the situations being observed and that different observers will use different procedures to record their observations.

Field experiments

In a field experiment researchers actively manipulate one of more aspects of the situation in a systematic way. It is an *experiment* rather than observation because at least one variable is manipulated (the IV) and then the researcher records their behaviour on a second variable (DV). Field experiments are used to control events that are infrequent to observe naturally. They are also used to investigate the limits of a response whilst controlling for antecedent conditions as well as consequences of any behaviour. Subjects of field experiments are more obviously aware that they are in a psychological study and thus more prone to reactivity effects.

One of the most famous examples of participant reactivity is a study now known as the 'The Hawthorne Effect' involving a series of experiments in the late 1920s and early 1930s at a Western Electric factory in Hawthorne, Chicago (McCambridge, Witton & Elbourne, 2014). The purpose of the study had been to address the effects of physical environment on productivity. The study recruited two different groups of workers at the factory. On one day they gave one of the groups improved lighting and found productivity increased compared to the control group. When they changed other factors in the work environment such as giving workers longer breaks they also found productivity to increase. The experimenters concluded that the workers' productivity was increasing due to others being concerned about their workplace as well as providing them opportunities to discuss changes before they were taken. It did not appear to be due to change itself as when the workplace was returned back to its original state, work productivity was found to be at its highest.

Data collection in observation studies

How to collect data

Qualitative research gathers information that is not in numerical form and will typically include descriptive data. This can include diary accounts, open-ended questions and interviews. Observational studies can include qualitative information, for example observations might be made on types of behaviour shown by a teacher during a classroom activity. In contrast, quantitative research gathers data in numerical form which can be put into categories or measured in units of measurement. Experiments usually yield numeric data as they involve some sort of measurement. Using the same example provided in observation with qualitative information, a quantitative approach might involve coding of four "frames" of classroom teacher-student interaction per hour of observation (the quantitative information).

Narrative record: Recording the behaviour of the subjects being observed exactly as it originally occurred. Researchers can organise the content of the recordings at a later date.

Videotape and audio recordings: Mechanical recording devices are generally not subject to bias in terms of the behaviours that get recorded. The researcher still needs to decide how and when they will make measurement or observations. There are ethical implications to using both audio and video recordings of children. Children and carers should give their permission to be videotaped/recorded.

When to collect data

The researcher has to make decisions about how to limit the information they are getting to restrict the quantity of data to something that is manageable for future analysis. Sampling refers to the method in which they choose to select this information. There are three methods of sampling: time, event and situation.

Time sampling: Record a behaviour at regular intervals over a period of time. For example, staff record what children are doing every 10–15 minutes over a 60-minute play session.

Event sampling: Recording an event whenever it occurs is useful for sampling infrequent behaviours.. For example, you may want to examine why or when a child shows aggressive behaviour. The ABC method is usually used to record the event. A is for Antecedent (triggers, behaviours and actions) before an event. B is for the Behaviour observed. C is for Consequences, what happens immediately after.

Situation sampling: The researcher chooses to observe the behaviour in more than one situation (for example location). This allows the researcher to generalise their findings to more than just one situation. It enhances the external validity of the study. If a child shows hyperactive behaviour both at home and at school, you are more likely to infer the child is hyperactive in temperament. If the child only shows the behaviour at school, you are more likely to infer that something in the school environment is contributing to their behaviour.

Coding the data refers to the process of assigning a different number to each category of the behaviour being observed.

- *Strengths:* Sample of natural behaviour, data can be recorded in different ways (event sampling, time sampling), it can be carried out in laboratory settings.
- *Limitations:* The method needs an adequate sample of child's behaviour, it is subject to influence of the observer and equipment, it can be hard to meet relevant criteria.

Survey methods

A survey can be either questionnaire based or conducted in interviews with a representative sample. Questionnaires offer researchers a quick and easy way to collect a great deal of information. One weakness of this method is that it reduces variety, creativity and individuality of responses. In cases where the subject is unable to fill out a questionnaire, with very young children for example, questions are often posed through a structured interview.

- *Strengths:* Effective for revealing broad patterns, it provides wide-reaching information.
- *Limitations:* Difficulty in generalising findings and provides limited detail.

Interviewing children

Interviews can allow researcher to get children's views directly. In unstructured interviews, children would talk about the subject of interest without a fixed set of questions being asked. For example, a researcher who is interested in what children look for in a friend may ask a couple of leading questions but allow the child in the interview to talk freely about their experiences. Follow-up questions by the researcher are led by what each child says. Interviews will differ greatly across the children being interviewed as the researcher improvises and follows leads of each individual conversation. In semi-structured interviews, the researcher uses a series of open-ended questions followed by specific probes to be able to generalise answers to questions across children. Questions are created beforehand based on child self-reports and observations of the child, and hypotheses surrounding the question being addressed. Structured interviews consist of a series of specific questions or statements, but this time the child's responses are structured as well. This can be using a 'Yes/ – No' choice or as a point on a scale ranging from 'Strongly agree' to 'Disagree'. For any interview to be valid the interview and questions must be tailored to the child's level of understanding.

- *Strengths:* Information is collected first hand from the individual, clinical interviews allows collection of a large amount of data, structured interviews are useful for children with short attention span, questionnaires are useful for older and literate children.

- *Limitations:* Children may be unable to provide information, young children may provide wrong information, children may provide false memories, children may respond in socially desirable ways.

Third-party reporting

In order to address a question relating to development, a researcher may ask a parent or teacher via interviews or questionnaires. For example, if researchers are interested in how children's early language development predicts reading ability at school, they are likely to be reliant on parents to provide them information such as when the children started speaking, their first words, etc. In some cases third-party data is used in conjunctive with direct data from children. In the case of whether children show more aggressive behaviours at home or school, the researcher can directly observe the child in these environments as well as collecting data from parents and teachers. However one of the major criticisms of research from third parties is that the information often fails to gain an insight to how the child views the problem.

- *Strengths:* Teachers and carers may also be able to accurately comment on the behaviour of child, data from one person can be used together with data collected using another method.
- *Limitations:* Parents and teachers may be biased, they may not remember episodes, they may be susceptible to social desirability effects.

Psychophysiological models

This includes the physiological bases of psychological processes. Many measures are part of modern psychophysiology including measures of brain activity such as brain responses to specific events (event-related potentials, ERPs), brain waves (electroencephalography, EEG), fMRI (functional magnetic resonance imaging), measures of skin conductance (skin conductance response, SCR; galvanic skin response, GSR), cardiovascular measures (heart rate, HR; beats per minute, BPM; heart rate variability, HRV; vasomotor activity), muscle activity (electromyography, EMG), electrogastrogram (EGG), changes in pupil diameter with thought and emotion (pupillometry) and eye movements, recorded via the electro-oculogram (EOG) and direction-of-gaze methods.

- *Strengths:* Establishes relationships between variables, useful for new areas or generating hypotheses.
- *Limitations:* Difficulty to generalise, intrusive, requires preparation and time.

Case study

A case study is an in-depth analysis of a particular individual. While this research method provides a great deal of information about a specific person, the results are often difficult to generalise to larger populations. For this reason, case studies are most often used in clinical research or other cases where certain aspects of the subject's life cannot be reproduced or duplicated. In Chapter 6 you will be introduced to case of Genie, a girl who spent the first few years of her life in extreme isolation and was unable to talk. In order for researchers to learn how she would develop language, she was followed for several years and researchers were able to include an in-depth investigation on different language measures. It would have been impossible to achieve this level of detail studying many participants due to time constraints.

- *Strengths:* In-depth investigation, useful for new areas or generating hypotheses.
- *Limitations:* Hard to generalise, very time consuming.

Standardised tests

A 'standardised' test is one given in the same way to every test taker. Many types of standardised tests are available for use with infants, children and adolescents. All are psychological tests whether they measure abilities, achievements, aptitudes, interests, attitudes, values or personality characteristics. These provide age norms to compare children's performance.

- *Strengths:* Objectively administered and scored, norms based on clearly defined populations
- *Limitations:* Narrow focus in what they can measure, shows only differences in number of behaviours.

Cross-cultural studies

Examining behaviour and mental processes of children in different cultures helps determine the degree of generalisability of findings.

Important environment influences for differences in behaviour are able to be addressed. An example is attachment behaviours, the bond formed between the infant and caregivers in the first few months of life. As we will see in Chapter 9, there have been four attachment behaviours identified in children following separation and then reunion with caregivers (secure, insecure ambivalent, insecure avoidant and disorganised). The four attachment types have been found in all cultures with most cultures showing two-thirds of children display secure attachment styles (Van IJzendoorn & Kroonenberg, 1988). However some cultures or countries are different. In Japan, children are more like to develop an insecure ambivalent style, whereby children are extremely distressed after being left by their parents, due to different rearing patterns that occur as part of the Japanese culture (Rothbaum, Weisz, Pott, Miyake & Morelli, 2000).

- *Strengths:* Helps to generalise results, shows the effect of environment.
- *Limitations:* Introduces more variability.

Summary of data collection methods

- Observational methods: naturalistic observation; structured observation; field experiments
- Survey methods
- Interviewing children: unstructured; semi-structured; structured
- Third-party reporting
- Psychophysiological models
- Case studies
- Standardised tests
- Cross-cultural studies

Research design

A research design refers to the overall strategy chosen by a researcher in order explore various aspects of a question in a coherent and logical way. Various research designs can be used to study issues of child development. Each design has advantages and disadvantages. In this section we concentrate on explanatory research using experimental research designs.

Experimental research involves a study in which a treatment, procedure, or program is intentionally introduced and a result or outcome is observed. The aim is to develop an answer to the 'Why' question, through discovery, elaboration or amendment of a causal relationship.

True experiments have four elements: manipulation, control, random assignment and random selection. The most important of these elements are manipulation and control. Manipulation means that something is purposefully changed by the researcher in the environment. Control is used to prevent outside factors from influencing the study outcome. When something is manipulated and controlled and then the outcome happens, it makes us more confident that the manipulation 'caused' the outcome. In addition, experiments involve highly controlled and systematic procedures in an effort to minimise error and bias to increase our confidence that the manipulation 'caused' the outcome.

Another key element of a true experiment is random assignment. Random assignment means that if there are groups or treatments in the experiment, participants are assigned to these groups or treatments randomly (for example, through the flip of a coin). This means that whoever the participant is, he/she has an equal chance of getting into all of the groups or treatments in an experiment. This process helps to ensure that the groups or treatments are similar at the beginning of the study so that there is more confidence that the manipulation (group or treatment) 'caused' the outcome.

A control group in a scientific experiment is a group separated from the rest of the experiment where the IV being tested cannot influence the results. This isolates the IV's effects on the experiment and can help rule out alternate explanations of the experimental results.

Matched-subjects design

A matched-subject design uses separate experimental groups for each particular treatment, but relies upon matching every subject in one group with an equivalent in another. The idea behind this is that it reduces the chances of an influential variable skewing the results by negating it.

Matched-subjects designs are often used in education, giving researchers a useful way to compare treatments without having to use huge and randomised groups. For example, a study to compare two new methods for teaching reading uses a matched-subject research programme. The researchers want to compare two methods, the current method and a modern method. They select two groups of children and match pairs of children across the two groups according to ability, using the results of their last reading comprehension test. If the researchers wanted to test another method, they would have to find three comparable groups.

Within-subjects, between-subjects designs

A within-subjects design is an experiment in which the same group of subjects serves in more than one treatment (IV). All children take part in the same studies. In a **between-subjects design** each participant participates in one and only one group. The results from each group are then compared to each other to examine differences, and thus, the effect of the IV. The reading method example above is a between-subjects design. If the researcher had chosen to use within-subjects design for that trial, all students would be taught first one method, then the other. The researcher could choose to measure comprehension at the beginning and end of each method and compare rates of individual improvement. There are a number of issues to consider in deciding whether an experimental factor should be assigned within subjects or between subjects.

Sometimes there is no choice. If for example, gender is a factor in an experiment, the experimental variable must be assigned between subjects, because a participant cannot be both male and female. Gender must be a between-subjects factor, with separate groups of male and female recruited for the experiment. Conversely, if an experiment seeks to investigate the acquisition of skill over multiple sessions of practice, then the only option for the factor session is within subjects. However, in many other situations, there is a choice. Take the following example: a researcher wants to investigate types of exercise on children's memory. How could a within- and a between-subjects design be used?

A within-subjects design example

A researcher is interested discovering whether different types of exercise have different effects on a child's memory. Two types of exercise are chosen: aerobic exercise and anaerobic exercise. The experiment is designed so that in the 'aerobic' condition they have participants run for five minutes, after which they take a memory test. In the 'anaerobic' condition they have *the same* participants lifting weights for five minutes, after which they take a different memory test of equivalent difficulty.

The researcher compares the childrens' performance on the two memory tasks to see whether any difference in memory ability is shown after the two types of exercise.

Strengths: There are two fundamental advantages of the within-subjects design: (1) power and (2) reduction in error variance associated with individual differences. Since you have the same subjects in both groups, you will have twice as many 'subjects' then if you had used a between-subjects design.

In a between-subjects design, even though you can randomly assign subjects to groups, the two groups may still differ with regard to important individual difference factors that affect the dependent variable. With within-subjects designs, the conditions are always exactly equivalent with respect to individual difference variables since the participants are the same in the each condition. So, in our exercise example above, any factor that may affect memory, such as sleep the night before, intelligence or memory skill, will be exactly the same for the two conditions, because they are the exact same group of people in the two conditions

Weaknesses: There is also a fundamental disadvantage of the within-subjects design, which can be referred to as carryover effects also known as 'order effects'. In general, this means the participation in one condition may affect performance in other conditions, thus creating a confounding extraneous variable that varies with the independent variable. Two basic types of carryover effects often seen are the positive effect of practice and the negative effect of fatigue. One way to control for order effects is to counterbalance the order in which the children complete the tasks. For example, some children will do the aerobic exercise first followed by anaerobic and others will do the opposite.

Using a between-subjects design may be a way of avoiding the carryover effects that can plague within-subjects designs. In this same example one group would be allocated to aerobic exercise and the other to anaerobic exercise. However it may be that that one class of children were much sportier than the other class, a factor that would undermine the validity of the experiment. To avoid this, randomisation and matched pairs are often used to smooth out the differences between the groups. Children could be randomly allocated to conditions to spread the extraneous factor such as whether children who regularly take part in a sports activity, ensuring they are not all in one group. Alternatively children could be matched to ensure both groups have children with similar level of sports activity in each.

Between-subjects designs are invaluable in certain situations, and give researchers the opportunity to conduct an experiment with very little contamination by extraneous factor. Disadvantages are that between-subjects designs can be complex and often require a large number of participants to generate any useful and analysable data. Because each participant is only measured once, researchers need to add a new group for every treatment and manipulation. It is not only difficult to find enough participants to be able to generalise results, but individual variability is also still likely to exist in all groups. Age, gender and social class are just some of the obvious factors but intelligence, emotive quotient and every other personality construct can influence the data. Trying to measure and match these characteristics beforehand could mean a subject population is impossible to collect. On the other hand, problems trying to generalise results can arise if all of the subjects are of the same age, gender and background, as you may not then be able to extrapolate the results to encompass wider groups.

Experimental designs

- *Strengths:* Allows identification of causal relationships between two or more variables.
- *Limitations:* Findings from carefully controlled laboratory studies may not generalise to real world settings.

◉ Correlational research

Correlational research investigates the relationship between two variables in a single population to determine if they are associated. Correlational research helps provide child psychologists with important information about the possible cause and effect for various issues, however, just because two variables are *correlated* does not prove that one *causes* the other.

Correlational research provides three possible results: positive correlation, negative correlation and no correlation. A positive correlation indicates that both variables increase or decrease at the same time. For example, a positive correlation between a measure of the quality of parent–child relationship and a measure of the social-emotional development of a the child would indicate that as the quality of the parent–child relationship measure increases then so does the social emotional development of the child measure. A positive correlation would also show that as the quality of the parent–child relationship decreases, so does the social emotional development of the child. Negative correlation indicates that as the amount of one variable increases, the other decreases. So for example, if researchers found that measurements of the child's social-emotional development decreased as the quality of the parent–child relationship measure increases (or vice versa) then a negative correlation would be indicated. Finally, if the researchers found that there was no discernable pattern to the results of measuring social-emotional development in children and the quality of the parent–child relationship, then a result of no correlation would be indicated

The level of correlation can be indicated using a numbers on a scale. The numbers that indicate correlational strength are called correlation coefficients. The most famous is the Pearson correlation coefficient which ranges from -1.00 to $+1.00$. A correlation coefficient value close to -1.00 indicates a strong negative correlation, while a coefficient close to $+1.00$ indicates a strong positive correlation. A correlation coefficient of zero indicates no correlation.

- *Strengths:* Analyses the relationship between a large number of variables in a single study group, the correlation coefficient gives a measure of degree and direction of the variables relationship.
- *Limitations:* No cause-and-effect relationship can be established, breaks complex relationships into too simple components.

◉ Elements of time in research design

Development is a process of change over time. Therefore aspects of time are particularly important considerations for developmental psychologists when planning the research investigation (Miller, 1993). There are several approaches available to psychologists, including studying different individuals of different ages and compare them, or studying the same individuals as they age over time and a combination of these approaches. The next section discusses four common research designs:

- Cross-sectional designs
- Longitudinal designs
- Microgenetic designs
- The time-lag design

Cross-sectional studies

This type of study selects different groups of people who differ in the variable of interest, but are similar on all other factors such as SES and ethnicity. For example, a group of people might be selected that only differ on the variable of interest (age) in order to attribute any effects to age. These studies occur at a single point in time and do not involve manipulating variables. Instead they are observational in nature and so provide only descriptive data. They are useful to make hypotheses about further research such as prevalence of something in a population but are not able to determine cause–effect relationships. However, the requirement for a unique group of individuals who differ on only one variable can potentially reduce the number of people available to take part in the study. Also the population may be exposed to problems of cohort effects, for example people born in same time period may be impacted by important historical experiences not shared by earlier or later generations.

- *Strengths:* Most efficient way of studying age-related changes, useful for studying group differences, allows researchers to look at numerous things at once.
- *Limitations:* Fails to address issues about individual children, problems of cohort effects.

Longitudinal studies

In contrast to cross-section which features on one defined time period, longitudinal studies involve taking multiple measures of a variable over a long period of time, for example, measuring the behaviour of the same set of children at different ages and comparing the results. Longitudinal studies present more opportunities for the researcher to obtain insight on patterns of stability/instability of multiple individuals over time. However, due to time constraints of a longitudinal design a small number of observations are usually collected on widely spaced time intervals. The longer the gap between time intervals the harder it is to capture the on-going process of change.

- *Strengths:* Study individual differences across time, identifies developmental pathways, provides information about developmental change, identifies how dependent variables change as a function of age of birth cohort effects.

- *Limitations:* Require a great deal of time, problems of cohort effects, practice effects, participation withdrawal.

Microgenetic designs

In both cross-sectional and longitudinal designs the researchers see the products of change but not the actual process (Kuhn, 1995). Microgenetic designs are specifically designed to closely observe process of change instead of the actual result (Lavelli, Pantoja, Hsu, Messinger & Fogel, 2005) They look at moment-to-moment change within a short period of time (weeks, months) but typically during rapidly changing developmental periods. Regardless of the developmental domain of interest, there are key characteristics that define all microgenetic designs.

1 Individuals are observed through a period of change.
2 Observations take place before, during and after change in a particular domain occurs.
3 Observations are conducted at time intervals that are considerably shorter than the time intervals required for the developmental change to occur.
4 Observed behaviours are subjected to both quantitative and qualitative analysis.
   - *Strengths:* Fine-grained analysis of developmental change, gives a more complete picture of rapid change.
   - *Limitations:* Can be subject to practice effects.

Time-lag designs

Time-lag design allows a researcher to see differences in behaviour associated with particular ages at various times in history. That is, instead of focusing on one cohort or one time of measurement, the time-lag design considers only one age level and looks at the characteristics associated with being a particular age at different times in history. For example, a researcher may measure levels of aggressive behaviour in 13-year-olds over a period of ten years. Every year for ten years she/he conducts the same measurements on a population of 13-year-olds. A time-lag design aims to investigate time effects on certain dependent variables with age being constant. Consequently subjects at different times of investigation stem from different cohorts. For example, 13-year-olds in 1991 and 1996 were born in 1978 and 1983. That is, not time, but the time lag factor is varied with the steps time 1991/cohort 1978 and time 1996/cohort 1983. The study may illuminate the level of cohort effects or may help to illustrate aspects of development which stay stable while environmental variables change over time.

- *Strengths:* Can control cohort effects, useful as a supplement to longitudinal studies.
- *Limitations:* Fails to address individual differences, on its own, it only address cohort effects.

◉ Ethics in research design

Adhering to norms of ethical behaviour by researchers and institutions is important for many reasons. Beyond ethical norms relating to honesty, integrity, objectivity, competency, non-discrimination, legality and safety, there are particular requirements for researchers to conform to agreed ethical standards when conducting research with human subjects in order to minimise harm and maximise benefits of the research. All studies treat issues of research ethics in the same way to safeguard the children and their parents. Whether the researcher is using an observation study or the use of video and audio recordings of interviews, all studies seek to gain voluntary consent from the participants and to give participants the opportunity of withdrawing their data.

At the planning stage of the research we need to consider not only possible consequences of the misuse of the results but also the rights and needs of children participating in the research. Researchers must truly respect children's views (Morrow & Richards, 1996) as well as their freedom to take part (or not to take part). We also need to listen to and include the perspective of the child and young people in the research. Inviting freely and obtaining consent from all children participating in the research, and from the parent or guardian of those under 16 years old is important, while at the same time ensuring the child understands that they can refuse to answer any question or withdraw at any time.

There is a need to inform parents and children, using age-appropriate language in either letters or leaflets what the aims of the research are, how the data and/or results of the research will be disseminated and how their data will be stored. All data must remain confidential, removing all personal identifiers and assigning pseudonyms where possible. All data must be stored in accordance with any legal requirements of the country of research, for example the Data Protection Act (UK).

All researchers have a duty of care to inform the participants of any potential risks, to provide a debriefing after each research interview and to provide participants with the researcher's name and contact information. Providing feedback of the results to all who ask for it (schools or homes if requested) is also important. Most institutions conducting research on human or animal subjects have a research ethics committee or similar body which meets to consider planned research and ensure the design will meet their established ethical requirements. The American Psychological Association (APA) has guidelines that all researchers must follow when proposing and conducting behavioural research with animals and humans.

1 Minimise risk to research participants. If psychological and physical risks are unnecessary, they must be avoided.
2 Disclose the true nature of the research to all participants to determine participation; avoid deception.
3 Keep results anonymous and confidential. Do not share participants' information and identification.

Chapter 4

Biological Psychology

What role does genetic inheritance play in a child's development and how much is contributed by the environment? This question has puzzled scientists and psychologists for centuries, most frequently referred to as the nature (genetic background) versus nurture (our environment) debate.

Whilst it is impossible to account for every influence that determines a child's personality, there are key influences that have been identified in a child development including parenting styles, relationships with friend and family and experience in the home and at school. Most psychologists now consider that it is an interaction of both genetic and environmental factors that shape a child, with the genetic make-up laying the foundations to how the child develops with the environment. Their different environmental experiences will impact on how these foundations will ultimately be expressed, shaped or even suppressed.

In this chapter, we will examine:
- What biological influences shape a child's development?
- What are the key environmental influences?
- How do environment factors interact with genetics?
- The role of genetic disorders on a child's development

👁 Biological influences

The development of a child starts when the male reproductive cell, or sperm, penetrates the protective outer membrane of the ovum, the female reproductive cell. Both the sperm and ovum contain chromosomes that act as the blueprint for human life. These chromosomes hold a chemical structure known as DNA (Deoxyribonucleic acid) containing the genetic code that makes up all life. Both the sperm and ova each contain only 23 chromosomes. This ensures that when the two cells meet, the resulting new organism has the correct 46 chromosomes.

The genotype refers to all genes that are inherited whereas the phenotype determines the actual expression of these genes. The phenotype includes both physical and non-physical traits including the height and colour eyes of a person but also the child's temperament such as shy or anxious child. There are two factors that have been found to be important in determining how the genes are expressed: the interaction with other genes and also the influence of the environment on the genotype.

Genes often consist of conflicting information and will work in additive ways whilst others battle for dominance. When working in an additive manner, the difference between the genes is split such that a 'tall' gene and a 'small' gene will be averaged out. In other cases genes follow a dominant–recessive pattern. Eye colour is a good example of this dominant–recessive battle. If one parent hands down a dominant brown eye gene whilst another parent hands down the recessive blue eye gene, the dominant gene will win resulting in a child with brown eyes.

However, the genetic blueprint can also be disrupted by environmental factors, starting when the child is in the uterus and continuing throughout life. Alcohol and drugs have frequently been shown to have an effect on a child's development. For example, exposure to alcohol during pregnancy can cause birth defects including those found in foetal alcohol syndrome. Consistent features of foetal alcohol syndrome are permanent and diminished physical growth, abnormal position of and function of joints is common, whilst facial deformities – such as flattening of the cheekbones and short nose – may also be present. Cognitive performance is often impaired with children showing signs of hyperactive behaviours and learning difficulties may be evident (Davis, Gagnier, Moore & Todorow, 2013).

Chronic illness can also impact on how the genetic code will manifest itself. Generally an illness is considered chronic when it persists for three months or more (Fritz & McQuaid, 2000); these can include asthma, cystic fibrosis, cerebral palsy and diabetes. Chronic illness need to be managed over a period of months, years or even the life course. Chronic illness comprises very diverse group of disorders and have different implications depending on the condition such that asthma and cystic fibrosis may show different side effects. Chronic illnesses are on the rise, in part because 90% of children diagnosed with one will now survive to age of 20 years (Pinzon & Jones, 2012).

A number of population studies show that children with a chronic illness are more at risk from internalising disorders such as anxiety and depression. They are more likely than their physically healthy peers to develop social and academic problems and to have poor social skills (Verhoof, Maurice-Stam, Heymans & Grootenhuis, 2013). They often fear rejection, develop insecurity in their academic ability and develop anxiety about how others will react to them.

◉ Physical development

Physical growth does not occur randomly but tends to follow orderly patterns known as cephalocaudal and proximodistal development (Duderstadt, 2013). The cephalocaudal pattern follows that growth occurs in a head-to-toe direction. For example, two months after conception, the human infant's head is very large in contrast to its total height. However, by birth the rate of growth in the rest of the body has begun to catch up. The head-to-toe direction of growth also explains why babies learn to hold their heads up before they learn to crawl. The proximodistal pattern reflects that development occurs outwards from centre of the body. For example, muscles of the neck are controlled before toes and fingers (Keenan & Evans, 2009). Larger muscles also develop before small muscles. For example, muscles in the body's core, legs and arms develop before those in the fingers and hands. This also explains why children achieve gross motor skills (e.g. walking) before they develop fine motor skills (e.g. drawing).

Body size (height and weight)

Children's development is tracked from the moment they are born. Measurements of a child's weight, height and head circumference are taken in the first few minutes of life and these measurements are then put onto an individual development chart mapping growth and development. Growth charts compare growth of children of similar age and gender as well as tracking patterns of child's height and weight growth over time. Growth charts use percentile bands to plot growth, with children in the 40th percentile for weight and length being heavier and taller than 40% of all other children of the same age and sex.

Most children's weight and height develops along similar lines. In the first year of life children grow dramatically, gaining ten inches (25 centimetres) in length and will triple their birth weight. After the first year of life, a baby's growth rate reduces considerably, and by two years of age growth in height usually continues at a steady pace of approximately two and a half inches per year until puberty.

A major growth spurt happens in puberty, with puberty typically lasting between four to five years. The growth spurt is associated with sexual development and includes the appearance of pubic and underarm hair, growth and development of sex organs and menstruation in girls (Brooks-Gunn & Ruble, 2013). The first sign of puberty in girls is breast buds, which can start anywhere between 8–14 but will typically start around 11, and periods following two years after breast buds start. Girls typically start their growth spurt early in puberty and will have done a lot of growing by the time their periods have started. They usually finish growing about the age of 15. The growth spurt happens much later for boys, usually around the age of 14, and their final height is not reached until age 17 or later. Puberty is also a time of significant weight gain; 50% of adult body weight is gained during adolescence (Lee & Styne, 2013).

Twin and adoption studies have consistently shown that there exists a strong genetic regulation of height and weight from infancy into adulthood. For example, a large-scale Danish study found that body mass index (BMI) of adoptive children from 7 to 13 years of age correlated more strongly with that of biological relatives than adoptive relatives, suggesting that genetic factors are more important than common environmental factors (Sørensen, Holst & Stunkard, 1992). In a recent study of 3,375 pairs of Australian twins and siblings, the heritability of height was found to be 80% (Visscher et al., 2006). On average, children of small parents will eventually attain lesser height than children of taller parents.

Genes versus environment

Whilst genes play a huge role in predetermining a child's size, other factors have an impact on how much a child grows. A good illustration is shown in a recent longitudinal study addressing the effect of genetic and environmental factors on height and BMI, based on maternal reports at 3, 5, 7, 10 and 12 years of age of a cohort of 7,755 pairs of Dutch twins.

The first-born twin was taller until age 10 and heavier until age 12 than the second co-twin. Heritability estimates were high for height (58–91) and BMI (31–82) but common and non-shared environmental factors were important also, becoming more so as the twins got older (Silventoinen et al., 2007). Non-shared environmental factors are defined as those that produce behavioural differences among siblings living in the same household.

Nutrition

Growth is highly dependent on our nutritional intake. Worldwide, the single most common cause of growth retardation is poverty-related malnutrition. Chronic malnutrition is characterised by delayed growth and the child will be considerably shorter than a normal height for their age. Acute malnutrition is characterised by insufficient weight in relation to the child's height (emaciation). Malnutrition also impacts upon puberty. Low nutrition is associated with a later start to menstruation where as a moderate degree of obesity is associated with early sexual maturation (Rogol, Clark & Roemmich, 2000). Adolescents with delayed puberty may fail to acquire bone mineral normally and have reduced bone mineral density as adults.

Physical activity

Although moderate activity is associated with cardiovascular benefits and favourable changes in body composition, excessive physical activity during childhood and adolescence may negatively affect growth and adolescent development. For example, it has been found that particular sports that restrict food intake and burn off excessive calories – like wrestling and gymnastics – may lead to growth problems. The body fails to take in the necessary nutrients it needs (Rogol, Roemmich & Clarke, 2002).

Hormones

Hormones control many of the physical changes that are observed at puberty. Hormones are chemical substances made by special glands and which pass all over the body through the bloodstream. The most important gland is the pituitary, located near the base of the brain. These glands trigger changes directly via the hormones they secrete into the bloodstream producing growth, but also indirectly by triggering other glands to release different hormones. Many of the physical changes, specifically sexual characteristics are controlled by the pituitary gland.

The testis in the male and the ovaries in the female become active, and secrete testosterone or oestrogens respectively. These hormones are responsible for people developing from children into young adults (Petersen & Taylor, 1980).

Recent studies of early versus late maturation have confirmed previous findings indicating that the impact of pubertal timing differs between boys and girls. Late-maturing boys have relatively lower self-esteem and stronger feelings of inadequacy, whereas early-maturing boys are more popular and have a more positive self-image (Petersen & Crockett, 1985). At the same time, however, early-maturing boys are at greater risk for delinquency and are more likely than their peers to engage in antisocial behaviours, including drug and alcohol use, truancy and precocious sexual activity (e.g., Williams & Dunlop, 1999). This increase in risky behaviour is likely due to an early maturer's friendships with older peers (Silbereisen, Petersen, Albrecht & Kracke, 1989).

Recent research on the timing of puberty among females also has confirmed previous studies indicating that early-maturing girls have more emotional problems, a lower self-image and higher rates of depression, anxiety and disordered eating than their peers (e.g., Ge, Conger & Elder, 1996). Interestingly, girls' perceptions of their maturational timing relative to peers may be more influential than their actual physical maturation (Dubas, Graber & Petersen, 1991). Like early-maturing boys, early-maturing girls are more popular, but they are also more likely to become involved in delinquent activities, use drugs and alcohol, have problems in school. Although there is little evidence that psychological difficulties stem directly from hormonal changes at puberty, it is likely that the bodily changes of adolescence play a role in the development of depression and disordered eating among girls (Wichstrøm, 1999). As body mass increases during puberty, adolescent females may develop a more negative body image and, in turn, disordered eating and depression (Keel, Fulkerson & Leon, 1997).

👁 Motor development (fine versus gross)

The preschool years are the period when young children acquire basic motor skills. The skills fall into two categories: fine motor and gross motor. Gross (or large) motor skills involve the large muscles such as arms and legs and include skills such as walking, running and jumping.

When evaluating a child's motor skills strength, muscle tone, movement quality and range of movement are looked at. Gross motor skills allow individuals to become mobile and engage in skills requiring body movement. In contrast, fine (small) motor skills involve smaller muscles in the fingers, toes and eyes. Fine motor skills include more intricate actions such as writing, throwing and grasping of objects.

Gallahue (1993) proposed that children move through a developmental progression in the acquisition of motor skills. The sequence of the appearance of these phases is universal, although the rate of acquisition of motor skills varies from child to child (see Table 4.1 for an outline of the key physical development milestones and their approximate ages of acquisition). The reflexive movement phase ranges from birth to about

Age of acquisition (approx.)	Motor milestones
Newborn	Jerky, random uncoordinated reflexive movement
3 months	Head at 90 degree angle; uses arms to prop themselves up
5 months	Purposeful grasps; reaches for objects, transfers objects from hand to hand; stretching of body; plays with feet
7 months	Pushes head and torso off the floor; supports weight on legs
9 months	Gets to and from sitting; crawls; pulls to standing; eye–hand coordination
12 months	Walking
15 months	More complex motor skills
2 years	Learns to first climb up stairs and then down stairs
Preschool	Physically active cannot sit still; clumsy throwing balls Refines complex skills, hopping, jumping, climbing, running Improving fine motor skills and eye–hand coordination; cuts with scissors
School age	Uses physical activities to develop gross and fine motor control Motor and motor-perceptual skills better integrated

Table 4.1 Children's developmental motor milestones

one year of age. In this phase the infant engages in reflexive movements, actions that are initiated intentionally. The rudimentary movement phase includes the basic motor skills acquired in infancy: reaching, grasping and releasing objects, sitting, standing and walking. The skills of the rudimentary movement phase acquired during the first two years form the foundation for the fundamental phase. The fundamental movement phase occurs during the preschool years ranging from ages two to seven. During this phase, children gain increased control over their gross- and fine-motor movements. They are involved in developing and refining motor skills such as running, jumping, throwing and catching. Control of each skill progresses through initial and elementary stages before reaching a mature stage. Children in this phase first learn skills in isolation from one another and then are able to combine them with other skills as coordinated movement. The specialised movement phase begins at about seven years of age and continues through the teenage years and into adulthood.

Gallahue and Ozmun (1989) caution that maturity and physical activity alone do not ensure that children will acquire fundamental movement skills in the preschool years. Children who do not master these skills are frustrated and experience failure later in recreational and sports activities (Baker, Horton, Robertson-Wilson & Wall, 2003).

👁 Brain development

A newborn's brain is about 25% of its approximate adult weight. It grows dramatically before the ages of three, such that it produces billions of cells and hundreds of trillions of connections, or synapses, between these cells (Eliot, 2010). Powerful new imaging technologies have been developed to track intellectual and behavioural development linked to the brain during childhood. Studies tracking the maturation of the brain show that different parts of the brain grow at different times with intermittent growth spurts as well as periods of more gradual growth. Imaging studies have also shown that youth diagnosed with mental disorders show patterns of development different than in unaffected youth (Schnack et al., 2014). Research in animals has shown that early experience including the quality of early parental nurturing has measurable effects on the brain and later behaviour (Koe, Salzberg, Morris, O'Brien & Jones, 2014). Early experiences shape how the brain-based stress response system develops and can influence later stress resilience (Moutsiana et al., 2014).

◉ Twin and adoption studies

The great nature–nurture debate can be further tested using an assortment of family studies, twin and adoption studies, to test personality
traits in biological families and non-biological families. The concept of
twin studies to determine the influence of genes was originally the
brain child of Sir Francis Galton, a cousin of Charles Darwin, in the
early 19th century. He started by looking at how genetics influence intelligence. By studying twins raised together and those raised apart scientists can gain a better understanding of the contribution of genetics and
environment. Scientists can also study monozygotic (identical) and
fraternal twins (twins who share 50% of their genes) who are raised in
the same environment to also determine environmental influences.
Under the general principles is that if heredity underlies certain personality traits then this relationship is expected to be stronger in monozygotic twins. However, given that many people treat twins very similarly it
is difficult to discount environmental factors. By studying monozygotic
twins raised in different environments, scientists can be more confident
of the impact of genes.

Adoption studies are equally important as they provide an opportunity to study how similar a child is compared to non-biological parents.
If an adopted child shares more in common with their adoptive family, it
provides a stronger argument for environmental influences. One of the
most famous twin studies was known as the Minnesota twin study
(Bouchard, Lykken, McGue, Segal & Tellegen, 1990). They examined a
set of identical twins that were raised in separate environments. When
the twins met for the first time 40 years later, they all shared similar characteristics including temperament, multiple personality traits, social and
occupational interests and social attitudes. The Texas Adoption project
results also showed that adopted children to be more like their biological
parents than their adopted families.

Cognitive abilities such as intelligence have been shown to predict
educational attainment, income and health (Deary, 2000). Since the
1920s, twin and adoption studies have investigated the genetic and environmental origins of individual difference in cognitive abilities, revealing
heritability estimates of about .5 for general cognitive ability (Plomin,
DeFries, Knopik & Neiderhiser, 2013). Genetic influence on cognitive
abilities reveals a steady increase in the heritability of general cognitive
ability from childhood through adulthood (Haworth et al., 2010).

👁 Genetic abnormalities

It is not uncommon for genetic abnormalities to occur, when a sperm or ovum is formed the number of chromosomes may divide unevenly resulting in more or less than the normal 23 chromosomes, in some cases, about one in every 200 live births. The majority of neurodevelopmental disorders are caused by genetic abnormalities. A genetic disorder is an illness caused by abnormalities in genes or chromosomes, which are often present before birth. Most genetic disorders are quite rare and affect one person in every several thousands or millions. A genetic disorder may be caused by an inherited genetic condition in some people, by new mutations in other people, and by non-genetic causes in still other people.

Genes contain the information used by other parts of a cell to make proteins. Proteins are the body's building blocks. Each protein performs a specific job. They make up the structure of your organs and tissues and are needed for all of your body's chemical functions. Each gene contains information for making at least one protein. If this information is changed, then the cell may not be able to make that protein, or it may not be able to make a form of the protein that the body can use. There are four main genetic types of neurodevelopmental disorders.

Types of neurodevelopmental disorders

1 *Disorders that result from mutations in a single gene*. Examples are, phenylketonuria and fragile X syndrome. Fragile X occurs because the FMR1 gene is unable to make normal amounts of usable Fragile X Mental Retardation Protein, or FMRP.

2 *Chromosomal disorders in which an entire chromosome is missing or deleted*. Examples are Down syndrome or Turner syndrome. Down syndrome occurs when there is an extra copy of chromosome 21. This form of Down syndrome is called Trisomy 21. The extra chromosome causes problems with the way the body and brain develop. Turner syndrome is a disorder that affects females only and is a chromosomal abnormality in which all or part of one of the sex chromosomes is absent (unaffected humans have 46 chromosomes, of which two are sex chromosomes). Normal females have two X chromosomes, but in Turner syndrome, one of those sex chromosomes is missing or has other abnormalities.

3 *Segments of a chromosome are either missing or duplicated.* Examples
are Williams syndrome or Prader–Willi syndrome. Williams
syndrome is caused by a deletion of about 26 genes from the long
arm of chromosome 7. Prader–Willi syndrome (abbreviated PWS)
is a rare genetic disorder in which seven genes (or some subset
thereof) on chromosome 15 (q 11–13) are deleted or unexpressed
(chromosome 15q partial deletion) on the paternal chromosome.

4 Another group of disorders is referred to as polygenic or complex
because they are assumed to be caused by several interacting genes.
These disorders (e.g., autism, specific language impairment or
dyslexia) typically involve inherited quantitative cognitive,
behavioural or personality traits (Tager-Flusberg, 1999).

Fragile X syndrome

Fragile X syndrome is a genetic condition involving changes in part of
the X chromosome. It is the most common form of inherited intellectual
disability (mental retardation) in boys. Fragile X syndrome is caused by a
change in a gene called FMR1. A small part of the gene code is repeated
on a fragile area of the X chromosome. The more repeats, the more likely
there is to be a problem. The FMR1 gene makes a protein needed for the
brain to grow properly. A defect in the gene makes the body to produce
too little of the protein, or none at all. Boys and girls can both be affected,
but because boys have only one X chromosome, a single fragile X is likely
to affect them more severely. You can have fragile X syndrome even if
your parents do not have it. A family history of fragile X syndrome,
developmental problems or intellectual disability may not be present.

Behaviour problems associated with fragile X syndrome include: delay
in crawling, walking or twisting, hand clapping or hand biting, hyperactive or impulsive behaviour, mental retardation, speech and language
delay, tendency to avoid eye contact. Not only do children with fragile X
syndrome share similar characteristic to children with an autism spectrum disorder (ASD) such as repetitive behaviours and lack of eye
contact, but many children also have a co-diagnosis of ASD (Belmonte &
Bourgeron, 2006). Some of the physical signs may include flat feet, flexible joints and low muscle tone, large body size, large forehead or ears
with a prominent jaw, long face and soft skin. There are very few outward
signs of fragile X syndrome in babies. Some signs may include large head
circumference in babies, intellectual disability, large testicles after the

start of puberty and subtle differences in face features. Importantly, genetic testing can diagnose this disease.

In brain-imaging studies it has been found that in fragile X syndrome many brain regions were enlarged, including the hippocampus, amygdale, caudate nucleus and thalamus; these areas are responsible for several cognitive functions including memory, learning, information and sensory behaviour (Hagerman, 2005). Two brain regions have also been found to be reduced; the cerebellar vermis which regulates motor control; and superior temporal gyrus, responsible of processing complex auditory stimuli.

Down syndrome

Down syndrome is a chromosome disorder caused by an additional copy of the whole or part of chromosome 21 usually in every cell. Trisomy 21, the chromosome abnormality responsible for 95% of Down syndrome (DS), is also considered to be one of the most important genetic causes of intellectual disability in humans, occurring in approximately one in every 600–800 live births (Hassold & Sherman, 2000). DS is a genetic condition that impacts upon development through life and is one of the most common causes of mild to moderate learning disability. Commonly it is characterised by impairments in cognitive ability and physical growth, as well as a particular facial characteristics. Common physical features include flat face, an abnormally small chin, round face, protruding/oversized tongue, shorter than normal limbs and poor muscle tone. There are also a number of health risks associated with DS including a higher than normal risk of congenital heart disease, sleep apnoea and reoccurring ear infections and thyroid dysfunctions as well as a weakened immune system and a heightened risk of early-onset dementia. Aside from the physical characteristics, problems with understanding and expressing speech are present, fine motor skills are also delayed and lag behind gross motor skills.

Children may also have delayed mental and social development. Common problems may include impulsive behaviour, poor judgment, short attention span and slow learning. They also show indiscriminate friendliness and therefore do not fear strangers. Some abnormalities have been found in regions of the cortex, in the temporal lobe, in the hippocampal formation and the cerebellum. DS can result from several different genetic mechanisms which can result in vast differences in the signs and symptoms displayed in children only after birth do the severity of their symptoms become present. Older mothers have a higher chance of having a baby with DS than younger mothers though children are born to parents of all ages, and all social, racial and economic backgrounds. The prognosis of the person is variable depending upon the possible complications like heart defects and leukaemia. Whereas in the early 1900s Down syndrome patients were expected to live to around ten years, 80% of adults with DS now reach their 50th birthday and beyond. Adults past the age of 50 are significantly more susceptible to dementia.

Williams syndrome

Also known as Williams–Beuren syndrome (WBS), Williams syndrome (WS) is a rare congenital abnormality, which is caused by the deletion of the gene that makes the protein elastin from chromosome 7. This protein is responsible for providing strength and elasticity to blood vessel walls. The syndrome leads to medical and developmental problems. It is not thought to be inherited, as the chromosome abnormality occurs randomly and is unpredictable.

Characteristic features of the face seen in all individuals include 'elfin' facial features: an upturned nose, widely spaced eyes, wide mouth with full lips, small chin and slightly puffy cheeks. Most individuals (98%) have cognitive impairment, a hoarse voice, and many of them (74%) have congenital heart problems. Hyperacusis (sensitivity to some frequency sounds) is also very common. WS's cognitive profile is characterised by relative strengths in language abilities, unusual or unexpected words occur in spontaneous conversation as well. For example, Bellugi remembers one time that an 11-year-old girl emptied a glass of milk in the sink saying, 'I'll have to evacuate it'. WS is present also with strengths in their social ability. Anecdotal reports convey the impression of people who have 'never met a stranger'. They are friendly and articulate and because of this it is very easy to overestimate their intellectual abilities. They remember people's birthdays, enjoy collecting things and love music (see work by Levitin, Cole, Lincoln & Bellugi, 2005).

Turner syndrome

Turner syndrome is a genetic condition found only in females and caused by an abnormal sex chromosome, one of the 23 pairs of chromosome a child is born with, which determines the baby's sex. It affects about one in every 2,000 girls. One of each pair chromosomes comes for each of a child's parents. In the sex chromosome the mother's contribution is always an X chromosome, while the father will contribute either an X or a Y. If the father provides an X, the result is XX and a baby girl; if the father contributes a Y, the baby will be XY and a boy. The Y chromosome determines maleness so if it is missing the child will be a female. A female with Turner syndrome has part or all of one X chromosome missing. 'Classic Turner syndrome' is referred to when one of the X chromosomes is completely missing. 'Mosaic Turner syndrome' is the X chromosome is complete in most cells but missing or partial in others. Two key characteristics of Turner syndrome include shorter than average height and underdeveloped ovaries leading to lack of periods and infertility.

Chapter 5

Cognitive Psychology

Early childhood is a time when children make marked progress in their mental development. Although less obvious to the eye than a child's physical growth, their cognitive development such as their thought processes, intellect and brain development are constantly growing. Children are steadily gaining new abilities in mental reasoning, cause and effect and these cognitive abilities are apparent from children solving a mathematical problem to a child simply understanding how to make a sound from a toy.

In this chapter, we will:
- Describe the three cognitive developmental theories (Piaget, Vygotsky and information processing)
- Highlight key studies in testing a child's cognitive development

Cognitive development refers to the development of thought processes or mental activity. This encompasses a wide array of abilities and skills including memory, attention, language, social cognition, reasoning, problem solving and more. Acknowledging the importance of cognitive development in a child's ability to learn and mentally grow, psychologists continue to study how and when the skills are acquired in order to cater the needs of children at home and in a school environment.

Two of the biggest contributors in our understanding of children's cognitive development, have been Jean Piaget (1896–1980) and Lev Semionovich Vygotsky (1986–1934). Both men were considered to be constructivists in that they both believed children learn by fitting new information together with what they already know. They both believed not only that learning is affected by the context in which the information was learnt, but that cognitive growth is controlled by societal influence.

Jean Piaget

Piaget put forward a theory that he believed was the blueprint to how a typically developing child develops his or her intellect, thoughts, judgement and knowledge, from infancy through to adulthood. It is considered the most important to emerge from the study of human development (Siegler, 1998) for three main reasons. It provides a remarkable 'feel' for what cognitive development looks like, is of interest to the layperson and is notable for its breadth.

Piaget argued that children actively explore their world, and their thoughts are constructed based on the child's interactions with the world. Children use schemata, an interrelated set of actions, memories, thoughts or strategies based on past experience, to help them predict and understand the environment. Central to his theory are two biological concepts, adaptation and organisation (Ginsburg & Opper, 1988).

- Organisation is the individual's tendency to organise their cognitive structures or schemata into efficient systems (Lutz & Sternberg, 1999).
- Adaptation involves the creation of cognitive structures or schemata through our interactions. Adaptation occurs via assimilation and accommodation (Piaget, 1952).

Figure 5.1 Demonstration of accommodation

Assimilation refers to the process of integrating information in the environment into one's current psychological structures. For example, a child may learn from their environment that an animal which has a mane, tail and four legs may be classified as a horse. Accommodation is the opposite process; it happens when a person's old information or schemata are adjusted to better fit with the information in the environment. For example when learning that the animal has black and white stripes, the person adapts previous knowledge to understand that the animal is not a horse but a zebra. Both these processes may operate simultaneously (Ginsburg & Opper, 1988).

When we assimilate changes in the environment we are in a state of cognitive equilibrium, a 'steady state' which the system aims to maintain. When we are forced to accommodate we enter into a state of cognitive disequilibrium, which enable us to modify our cognitive structure. Piaget referred to this continuous balance as equilibration (Piaget, 1952).

⊙ Piaget's stages of sensorimotor development

Piaget (1952) presented four stages that children would pass through depending on the age of the child.

1 Sensorimotor (0–2 years)
2 Preoperational (2–7 years)
3 Concrete operations (7–12 years)
4 Formal operations (adolescence through to adulthood)

Whilst children may pass though the stages at different ages, Piaget insisted that that the sequence of stages was the same for every child and that stages cannot be skipped due the earlier stages providing the skills for the later, more complex ones.

Sensorimotor stage

The sensorimotor stage is thought to span the first two years of a child's life. Infants initially understand the world via their actions with the world but are unable to think about these actions. Gradually, children will develop the ability to use symbolic representation during this stage. The end of the stage signals the start of make-believe play. According to

Piaget (1954), the major achievement of this stage is the development of object permanence.

The vast difference in the behaviours between a newborn and a two year old led Piaget to suggest that there are six sensorimotor sub-stages which develop in a set order.

At birth children have little knowledge about their world and are unable to purposefully explore it (Berk, 2011). Instead they are born with simple reflexes such as sucking, grasping and looking. These reflexes are important as they provide the building blocks for later sensorimotor behaviours. During the reflective schema stage, infants gain some control and practice reflex behaviours. Around one month primary circular responses occur, where infants repeat chance behaviours that lead to satisfying results (e.g., thumb sucking). They also begin to start anticipating events, stopping crying when they think they are about to be fed.

From four to eight months they begin to show secondary circular responses, where they combine single schemata into larger structures (e.g., repeatedly grasping leads to shaking a rattle). They become skilled at reaching and manipulating objects in order get something to happen as a result of their actions. Improved controlled allows the child to imitate others more effectively. However the child is still unable during this stage to imitate novel behaviours.

It is not until the coordination of secondary circular reactions that the child's actions become intentional and goal-directed as the children are able to coordinate existing schemata of objects to use them correctly (means and action sequences). Piaget provided an example whereby a child was shown a new toy which was then hidden under a cloth. The child was able to get the toy by pushing aside the cloth and grasping the toy. They are also able to intentionally modify their behaviour as evidence by their ability to imitate using an object in a novel way such as copying an adult to push a toy car for the first time.

Object permanence is the concept of knowing that an object still exists even if it is hidden. It requires the ability to form a mental representation (i.e. a schema) of the object. For example, if you place a toy under a blanket, the child who has achieved object permanence knows it is there and can actively seek it. Before this stage, the child behaves as if the toy has simply disappeared. Children with no object permanence will typically show the A not B search error: when an experimenter hides an attractive toy under box A within easy grasp of the child, the child will be able to look for it under A. After several trials when the child watches the toy be moved under box B, also within easy reach, the child will still look for it under A.

The idea that hidden objects cease to exist in the mind of the infant was challenged in the 1980s by a number of infant researchers, including Liz Spelke and Renée Baillargeon (Baillargeon, Spelke & Wasserman, 1985). They argued that the hiding games that Piaget had based his account on were simply too difficult for infants. Infants did not search accurately because the task demands had overwhelmed their ability to execute the retrieval successfully. These limitations may reflect immaturity of brain structures which support sub-goals of complex behaviours necessary for search. Spelke (1991) and Baillargeon (1995) claim that a more accurate evaluation of the infant's understanding of the physical world could be obtained by observing infants' responses to magic tricks. Rather than requiring the infant to act, they simply watch an event sequence involving objects and the amount of time they spend looking at it is measured. The 'violation of expectancy' paradigm, as it has become known, is based on the principle of the conjurer's trick, namely that a trick triggers an increase in the observer's attention because it contravenes an expectancy or belief about the physical world. A simple example is to place an object on a table, cover it with an occluder, and then remove the occluder to reveal either the object (possible condition) or an empty space (impossible condition). If infants understand that the object should continue to exist, then those infants who observe the impossible condition should look significantly longer than those who observe the possible event. Using this simple logic, a large number of studies using the violation of expectancy paradigm have been conducted revealing infant discriminations on an extensive range of physical attributes and properties.

At 12–18 months children show tertiary circular responses, infants begin to repeat actions and vary them in a deliberating exploratory manner. For example, a child learns to use a stick in order to help them reach further. This flexible action pattern allows children to imitate more complex behaviours. This ability to explore is what leads to object permanence, the ability to understand that object exists even when hidden. This allows a child to find an object hidden even if they have not seen where it has been hidden. They no longer show the A not B search error. In the final sub-stage occurring at 18–24 months ages, children rely less on trial and error and are more likely to arrive at solutions straight away. Children become better at organising their experiences in meaningful and memorable units through images (mental pictures of objects, people and spaces) and through concepts (categories in which similar objects or events are grouped together). They solve advanced object permanence tasks – finding a toy in a location when they have not seen the object moved. They imitate behaviour even when behaviour of models is not present making possible make-believe play in which children act out everyday and imaginary activities. This is also the age in which a child develops a sense of self.

Preoperational stage

Language development is one of the key hallmarks of this stage. Children learn through imitation but cannot mentally manipulate objects and remain unable to take other people's point of view. Key features of the preoperational stage are the following.

1 The growth of representational abilities
Children become increasingly adept at using symbols, as evidenced by the increase in playing and pretending. For example, a child is able to use an object to represent something else, such as banana as a telephone. Role playing also becomes important during the preoperational stage.

2 Egocentrism
A child has a tendency to think only from his/her perspective, unaware that another person sees or thinks differently. Piaget used a number of creative and clever techniques to study the mental abilities of children. One of the famous techniques to demonstrate egocentrism was the 'Three Mountain Task', using a three-dimensional display of a mountain scene. Children are asked to choose a picture that showed the scene they had observed. Next they are asked to select a picture showing what someone else would have observed when looking at the mountain from a different viewpoint. Children at this stage typically select their own view on both occasions.

3 Animistic thinking
As a result of the child's egocentrism, children also believe that non-living objects have lifelike qualities such as thinking, feeling and acting like humans, e.g. 'The chair is mad, it tripped me up'. Children at this stage find it difficult to classify objects such as cars, plants, grass or a toy into living and not living. Whereas older children are able to make these differentiations.

4 Inability to perform mental operations, such as reversibility or **conservation tasks.**

During this stage the child's thinking is 'irreversible' in that the child cannot appreciate that a reverse transformation would return the material to its original state, for example to be able to imagine that a ball of clay that has been squashed could be made round again. Reversibility is a crucial aspect of the logical (operational) thought of later stages. Conservation is the understanding that an object's quantity stays the same even if its shape changes (see Concrete operation section below for an example of a typical test for this operation).

5 Centration

Children are able to focus on only one aspect or dimension of problems. For example, suppose you arrange two rows of blocks in such a way that a row of five blocks is longer than a row of seven blocks. Preoperational children can generally count the blocks in each row and tell you the number contained in each. However, if you ask which row has more, they will likely say that it is the one that makes the longer line, because they cannot simultaneously focus on both the length and the number. The ability to solve this and other 'conservation' problems signals the transition to the next stage.

Concrete operations stage

An operation is a rule-following transformation which we can make using our mental representations. In other words it is a type of logical thought process. Examples of operations include arithmetical operations such as

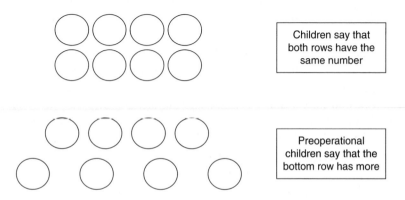

Figure 5.2 An example of centration

adding, subtracting, multiplying and dividing. The ability to conserve requires mental operations including reversibility – the understanding that a transformation can be un-done – and compensation – the recognition that one change will be compensated for by another, for example flattening a ball of clay will make it thinner but larger in area. Another example of an operation is converting a statement into its opposite, as illustrated by the child who said, 'When I grow down I want to be small'. During the stage of concrete operations, children can perform mental operations with real situations only.

This ability to perform operations means that children at this stage succeed in the conservation tests of the previous stage. Conservation tasks test a child's ability to see that some properties are conserved or invariant after an object undergoes physical transformation, such as a row of coins being stretched out, or a spherical lump of clay being rolled into a tube. Piaget's most famous task, the conservation of liquid (there are many others, e.g. conservation of substance, weight, number, etc.), involved showing a child two beakers, both of which were identical and which contained the same amount of coloured (typically blue) liquid. The child was asked whether the two beakers had the same amount of liquid in both. Then liquid from one of the glasses was poured into a taller, thinner glass. The child was then asked whether there was still the same amount of liquid in both glasses. A child who cannot conserve would answer 'No, there is more in the tall thin glass'.

Children at this stage can also manage seriation tasks. This means they can put concrete objects (or their representations) in order. For example if you told a child that Jonathan is taller than his brother Thomas, who is taller than their sister Kate, they could tell you which child was shortest. Children in this stage can also perform transitivity operations – these involve making new deductions from information given. For example, given the information about the three children above, they could correctly answer the question, 'Is Jonathon shorter or taller than Kate?'

They can also demonstrate the ability to make a flexible grouping of objects into classes and subclasses, allowing them to solve class inclusion problems. As an example of this test, Piaget and Szeminska (1941) showed children 20 wooden beads. Eighteen were brown and two were white. Each child was asked several questions:

1 Are all the beads wooden?
2 Are there more brown beads or white beads?
3 Are there more brown beads or more wooden beads?

Children in earlier stages cannot answer the third question correctly, with most children saying brown. They have problems with categories that overlap. However children who have reached the concrete operations stage are able to solve the problem.

This stage is also characterised by the decrease and elimination of egocentrism. The child can now distinguish between their perspective and that of others. Their thinking is still concrete, the ability to solve hypothetical problems is not developed yet.

Formal operations stage

Preadolescents and adolescents begin to understand abstract concepts and to develop the ability to create arguments and counter-arguments. They can apply operations not only to concrete situations, but also to abstract concepts that may have been invented or being hypothetical. For example, many psychological concepts are abstract. Adolescents also begin to think hypothetically. This means they can suggest what might be the result if something were to happen. For example, being able to say what might happen if all the polar ice melted.

The stage of formal operations also features greater flexibility in thinking. For example, adolescents are able to try one way of solving a problem, and then if it is unsuccessful, they discard it and think of another way. They have a range of strategies instead of being limited to one approach. For example, Piaget used to give participants some string and some weights which could be attached to the string, and to use these to find out what factor or factors determine how fast the pendulum swings. Participants can vary the length of the pendulum string, and vary the weight. They can measure the pendulum speed by counting the number of swings per minute. To find the correct answer, the participant has to grasp the idea of the experimental method – that is to vary one variable at a time (e.g., trying different lengths with the same weight). A participant who tries different lengths with different weights is likely to end up with the wrong answer.

This stage is viewed by Piaget as the endpoint of cognitive development. The child has achieved the ability to reason in propositional, abstract and hypothetical ways.

Strengths of Piaget's theory:

- Developed a wide array of information across different domains under one theory
- Stimulated a vast number of research studies
- Responsible for pushing cognitive development forward

Criticisms of Piaget's theory

- Reliance on verbal interview methods
- Conception of development as occurring in stages (Brainerd, 1978)
- Proposed universality (Rogoff, 1998)
- Concepts such as assimilation and accommodation are too vague (Brainerd, 1978)
- Development may not occur in a domain-general fashion (Gopnik & Wellman, 1994)

◉ Vygotsky's sociocultural theory of cognitive development

Vygotsky believed that all children are born active explorers and their social environment, namely their social interactions, are pivotal to the development of mental functions. His concepts are related to cognitive learning zones. The Zone of Actual Development (ZAD) occurs when children complete tasks on their own. The child is independent of others and needs no help in learning. In contrast, the Zone of Proximal Development (ZPD) requires adults or peers to provide assistance to the child (Blake & Pope, 2008). The ZPD is the difference between the child's actual developmental level (as determined by independent problem solving), and their potential development (as determined through problem solving under adult guidance or in collaboration with more capable peers). Instruction and learning occurs in the ZPD (Vygotsky, 1978, 1987).

Two important features of Vygotsky's learning zones are that capable members of a culture are able to assist others in learning, and that learning can be taken under guidance of others. The process of scaffolding (Bruner, 1983; Wood, Bruner, & Ross, 1976) is another important concept. Scaffolding is 'a form of adult assistance that enables a child or novice to solve a problem, carry out a task or achieve a goal which would be beyond his unassisted efforts' (Daniels, 2001).

According to Wertsch (1991) the three main themes from Vygotsky's theory are that:

1 Study of development must rely on 'generic analyses'
2 Cognitive development is largely a social process
3 Human cognitive ability is mediated by symbolic 'tools' such as art, numbers and language

Language and play

Vygotsky believed play, particularly pretend play, to be a critical part of childhood. He believed play to have an important role in a child's cognitive and social development. For example, Vygotsky (1984, 1987) believed children's speech to themselves during pretend play was a powerful means of regulating own behaviour. It provides children the means to reflect, organise and control their behaviour. It also allows children to develop abstract thought. For instance, Vygotsky explained, when a child can pretend that a broomstick is a horse, he or she is able to separate the object from the symbol. Vygotsky also believed that pretend play was also an important context in which children learned about their social world.

Educational implications

- Social interactions with more experienced others are essential to our education.
- Reciprocal teaching has been developed. Here, peers foster dialogues about a subject within their zone of proximal development (Brown & Pallinscar, 1989).
- Also through cooperative learning. Here a child's learning environment is structured into small groups of peers who work together toward a common goal.

Criticisms of Vygotsky's theories

- Yet to receive same critical analysis as Piaget's (Miller, 1993).
- Almost exclusive focus on the cultural aspects of development.
- Fails to consider how children's developmental level serves to constrain or enhance their opportunities for participation in various contexts.
- It does not explain how people determine the goals of their collaborative efforts.

◉ Comparison of the theories

There are fundamental differences between the two theories. Whilst Piaget believed the individual was primary in the learning process, Vygotsky considered social aspect to be the most important. Piaget's theory is built around the child as an active learner constructing their own knowledge. In contrast, Vygotsky highlights outside social forces on a child's development rather than themselves being the active learners. Others are needed in order to move the child's cognitive development forward. Piaget's theory focuses on fixed stages whereas Vygotsky's theory is more fluid, an on-going repertoire of development.

◉ How important are these theories to applications?

Piaget's theory allows teachers to align teaching strategies with the child's developmental stages. Their goal is to help the individual construct knowledge whilst being aware of what a child within a particular developmental stage is likely to be able or unable to do. Vygotsky's theory proposes that we need contact with more knowledgeable others to move development forward. A more capable person, such as a teacher or peer, provides assistance to the student; so that the student is able to complete the task with assistance. This informs teachers that they should be explaining, modelling and using guided practice in the classroom.

The final cognitive model to be discussed is the information-processing model.

◉ Information-processing model of cognitive development

The wide-reaching impact of the development of the computer in the 1950s and 1960s also had an effect on cognitive theory. Some cognitive psychologists began to use the computer as an analogy to the way the human mind handles information. In the same way a computer takes in information and follows a program to produce output, this model of cognitive psychology sees the individual as a processor of information. The human mind is seen as a system that processes information according to set rules and limits. Changes in the way information is processed is often attributed to greater efficiency rather than a structural change.

Basic assumptions to this approach involved the following:

1 Information made available by the environment is processed by a series of processing systems (e.g. attention, perception, short-term memory).
2 Processing systems transform or alter the information in systematic ways.

3 The aim is to specify processes and structures of cognitive performance.

4 Information-processing in humans resembles that of computers.

The information-processing approach characterises thinking as the environment providing input data, which is then transformed by our senses. The information can be stored, retrieved and transformed using 'mental programs' with the results being behavioural responses.

An example of an information-processing system is attention. We can perceive several things in our environment, but our attention is drawn to different aspects of it, for example attending to the words on the page of book in front of us, whilst ignoring the sounds around us from the television. Even as adults our attention can easily be distracted, for example by someone coming into the room. What makes us attend to one thing and ignore another is called selective attention, and how many things we can attend to at the same time is called attentional capacity, the ability to pay attention to something and ignore distractions is something that develops with age, or in the information-processing model, a system that becomes more efficient. Researchers using this model analyse errors or inefficiencies detected in the system in order to try to understand the processes more deeply. If humans are considered information processors, it suggests that humans can only process a limited amount of information at a time without being overloaded.

However the analogy between human cognition and computer functioning is limited. Humans are influenced in their cognition by a number of conflicting emotional and motivational factors – context, social content and social influences tend not to be addressed by this model, which focuses instead on internal processes.

👁 Evaluating the use of cognitive theories

Cognitive theories provide an explanation of a child's conscious thinking. In all these theories children are active in the construction of their understanding. Both Piaget and Vygotsky highlight the importance of precise developmental changes. None of the theories take note of a child's individual development. The information processing account does not provide an adequate account of developmental changes in cognition and it fails to acknowledge the importance of unconscious thoughts.

Chapter 6

Language and Communication

Learning to speak is one of the biggest achievements of early childhood. This important tool presents children with new opportunities for social understanding, learning about the world and for sharing experiences. Spoken language development also provides the foundations for learning to read. Whilst language acquisition and reading are two distinct processes they have been shown to directly impact upon on each other. For example, language skills have been linked to later successful reading. Equally, pre-literacy and literacy activities can help further children's language competencies in both the preschool years and later schooling (Dickinson & Tabors, 1991). It is impossible to underestimate the importance of language to a child's development. There are many cases in everyday life where children who have difficulty understanding others and in expressing themselves, have been shown to suffer psychosocial and emotional adjustment problems (Cohen, Farnia & Im-Bolter, 2013). Children with delayed or disordered language are therefore at increased risk for social, emotional and behavioural problems. As well, research shows that most children who have poor reading skills at the end of their first year in primary school will continue to experience difficulties reading later on in life (Snow, Burns & Griffin, 1998).

In this chapter, we will examine:
- What is language?
- How can we measure early language development?
- Are there universal stages of language development?
- Is language purely the result of learning, or do children have an innate ability?
- What role is played by social interactions?

◉ What is language?

Language is often defined as the human capacity for acquiring and using complex systems of communication. Whilst communication is not unique to humans, animals are considered to use communication systems in a more stereotypical way than that used by humans. For example, bird-song appears to have much in common with human language. Birds have an innate system of calls, although their songs mostly develop as they learn through experience (Atkinson, 1996). Equivalent to babies babbling, young birds have a period of sub-song before they develop their songs further, and they have also been found to have a critical period in which they are able to learn their song (Fitch, Hauser & Chomsky, 2005). As children are able to learn different languages they are sufficiently exposed to, so too can some species of birds. For example, the bullfinch is able to pick up the songs of different species (Fromkin & Rodman, 1998). Communication in birds is also similar to that of humans in that they too use different dialects, intonation patterns and rhythms within the same species in different geographical locations (see Hedeager, 1992).

Studies of communication amongst dolphins have also revealed complex systems akin to human language. Bottle-nose dolphins have impressive memory for sounds and capacity for imitative learning. It has been shown that they emit whistles with different pitch contours while experiencing different states. For example, downward glide = distress, upward glide = search, rise-fall-rise-fall = excitement or irritation (Bonner, 1980). Dolphins also use vocalisations for echo–location (navigation, food location, object identification). Primates also use a wide variety of communication tools (olfactory, auditory, tactile, visual and vocal) with meaning depending on the social and environmental context, as well as the emotional state of the animal. For example, vervets produce several distinct alarm calls, signalling different kinds of predators, they react differently to dominant and subdominant members of their own troop, family and rival troop. Young vervets appear to generalise and are unable to produce calls until they reach a certain age upon learning the different calls for certain situations (Diamond, 1991).

When considering whether language can be defined as a uniquely human attribute, it is also important to consider our closest relative in nature, the ape (Aitchison, 1996). The earliest experiments with chimpanzees showed that whilst they appeared to understand many spoken words they were unable to produce articulated speech (Wardhaugh, 1993). Some researchers have taught apes to use American Sign Language (ASL), (Gardner & Gardner, 1969), others to use keyboards for symbols (Savage-Rumbaugh, 1986) and others plastic tokens varying in shape, texture, size and colour representing words (Premack, 1976). One of the most impressive demonstrations of language use by animals comes from the chimpanzee Washoe who was taught to use a version of ASL (Fouts & Mills, 1997). She was found to use a combination of signs similar to the telegraphic speech of very young children, showing a gradual increase in the length of sign combinations she was able to use. She was able to create new words using sign language, understood the distinction between proper and common nouns, used a classification system and was able to express her thoughts and needs and to talk about the past, things not present and places she could not see. She taught other chimpanzees ASL signs, and her infant Loulis managed to learn 50 signs simply by picking up signs from his mother. Whilst the signs were more immature than that seen in humans, deaf children have been able to communicate with her, and the immaturity of signs may be more to do with not being taught by a native signer (Hedeager, 1992). Washoe's trainers draw conclusions that the chimpanzee's capacity for language is similar to that of a human child although more suited to gestural communication. One of the main difficulties in interpreting the results of animals studies, is that it remains a possibility they learn a series of behaviours through repetition. They may be reproducing behaviours based on association rather than being able to truly understand and use language in different contexts.

Another commonality that exists between animal and human communication is the fact that language develops over a long period and is refined the more the child interacts with speaking or signing adults. Children reared in isolation are thought not to acquire language and the same has been shown for animals. Language further develops by imitating elders and by observing, imitating, and playing. 'Motherese', now more commonly known as 'parentese', is an exaggerated and simplified use of language which parents adopts to communicate with babies. Some animals have also been found to use a similar adaptation to their normal communication patterns around their young. For example, Rhesus monkeys make unique vocalisations called the 'grimey' when they are around their infants to get their attention (Handwerker, 2007).

◉ Language development

There are four main aspects of language. Linguistic competence is acquired once all four of these aspects are achieved.

Phonology (sound). Phonology is the study of sounds in a particular language. The phonology of each language differs from others. It also studies the rules of sound (phonemes are the basic unit of sound) and the way they are combined to form words (e.g., psychology), syllables (e.g., in-come-ing), and morphemes (e.g., thought; thought-ful; thought-ful-ly; un-thought-ful-ly).

Semantics (meaning). Semantics is the study of the meaning of language. Children learn that morphemes, words and sentences convey meaning by referring to events, people, objects, relationships, etc.

Syntax (grammar). Syntax is the study of the structure of language and how words can be combined to create grammatically correct sentences. It refers mostly to the rules of language and how knowledge of word order, grammatical inflections and function words allow us to derive meaning from a sentence. For example, recognition that changing the word order changes the meaning of what is described ('Sarah pushed Claire' vs. 'Claire pushed Sarah').

Pragmatics (social context). Pragmatics refers to the social and contextual details behind the utterances in the language, such as desires and intentions. It is related to how the language is used in a socially appropriate way (e.g., not to say 'That lady's very fat!', even if it is true).

◉ Measuring language

Infants have been shown to pay attention to language from birth. How can we assess such young children? One way is through habituation. For 30 years or so, researchers have been devising creative ways to answer questions about infant perception of different dimensions of speech. Because infants are not yet able to answer questions or to directly indicate preferences, researchers have identified something infants can do – suck – and have built studies around that ability. The premise is that infants suck harder to indicate preference or novelty. Results of these studies indicate that infants even a few days old show a preference for their mother's speech when compared to that of another woman (DeCasper & Fifer, 1980). They also prefer the prosody (the rhythms and tonal variation, sometimes referred to as the music of the language) of their mother's voice compared to another woman's voice when listening to voices with the phonetic information screened out. However, if the tape of their mother is played backwards, making the prosody 'unnatural' the infant no longer prefers the voice of the mother (there is a change in the sucking behaviour). These early studies also show that infants prefer speech in their native tongue compared to a language system not their own. When listening to tapes with the phonetic information filtered out, infants still prefer the prosody (change their sucking behaviour), of their native language (Butterfield & Siperstein, 1972).

Early language exposure plays a critical role in shaping the young brain. Babies are born with the ability to recognise familiar sounds and language patterns. Foetal hearing begins to develop at four months gestation and the nervous system starts functioning. At six months gestation the foetus responds to sounds by kicking and a quickening pulse, by seven months their hearing is fully developed and the foetus responds to both visual and aural stimulation. In a recent study, newborn babies only hours old were able to differentiate between the sounds of their native language and a foreign language (Moon, Lagercrantz & Kuhl, 2012).

◉ Stages of language development

There are great similarities in all human societies in terms of language development. Children progressively master the rules of sound, meaning and grammar and learn to combine words in ways which are acceptable and understandable within their community. The stages are described below and summarised in Table 6.1 which follows.

Prelinguistic stage

Crying

Babies produce at least three different cries – associated with hunger, anger and pain. Early cries are probably responses to physiological states rather than attempts to communicate. Adults then mould these cries into communication. By the adult's response to the child, the child learns which cry to give depending on what he or she wants (Gustafsson, Levréro, Reby & Mathevon, 2013).

Cooing/gurgling

This stage occurs from about two months. It is clear that from birth communication develops via interaction. Kaye (1982) describes a period of 'shared rhythms and regulations' where the parent builds on the biological rhythms of the baby to develop a mutual dialogue which will form the basis for the communication patterns seen in the adult world. This is taken from the child's lead, where by about one month they develop sounds that are incorporated into their crying patterns, e.g. 'oooo' which seems to grow out of pleasurable social interactions such as during bath time. Adult–infant interactions are thought to be different from adult–adult interactions in several key ways. For example, in adult–infant interaction there is close proximity, exaggerated facial expression and repetition. Constant eye contact allows the adult to maintain and get the best attention from the infant (Ekerman & Stein, 1990). At this stage, infant and mother/father are very closely tuned to each other's emotional state.

Babbling, echolalia

At six–nine months children produce more vowels and some consonants rather than just cooing and crying sounds. Even deaf infants babble. Babbling of syllable-like sounds allows child to practice making sounds, to group them and to be able to practice intonation. Echolalia is the frequent repetition of sounds – 'dadadada' or 'mumumumumum' is common at this stage. This is the time when the 'babble' sounds babies make in one language start to sound different from the sounds babies make in other languages.

Babies can shout for attention and spend time making noises when they are alone. They develop a range of behaviours directed at familiar people, and parents generally believe their infant's sounds are attempts to communicate and spend a lot of time inferring intention to the sounds/actions. This process certainly helps cement the infant into the parent's social system and gives an early example of scaffolding. Fogel (1993) describes the infant–adult interaction as one of 'co-regulation of intentions' where each elaborates on the other's actions/intentions. He equates this process to that of a jazz band – a process of improvisation as they communicate with each other in mutually enjoyable ways.

One-word (holophrastic) speech

When the first words appear, at around 12 months old, the child is considered to have moved out of the 'prelinguistic stage'. At first they may not sound like words (e.g., 'oof' may be used to refer to every animal). But they are considered to be words if the child uses them consistently in the presence of a particular object or situation. These have the function of naming or labelling people and objects in the child's environment. They also condense meaning. The baby may use holophrases, or one word, to express a whole idea (e.g., 'milk' may mean 'I want some milk' or 'I have just spilt my milk'). It can take three or four months after the emergence of the first words before vocabulary increases, but then acquisition is fast. Vocabulary rises from around 20 words at 18 months to around 200 words at 21 months. New words are typically object names (mummy, car, dog) and action names (look, gone), state names (lovely, red) and some function words (there, bye-bye).

Telegraphic speech

At around 18 months the child begins to combine words into simple two-word sentences. Although they use single-word utterances, the first sentences are described as telegraphic speech, where speech contains highly condensed meanings (e.g., 'Ben shoe' for 'That is Ben's shoe', or 'Put on my shoe'). Parents may expand or recast the child's telegraphic speech (expand = 'Doggie go' ... 'Yes, the doggie is going away'; recast = 'doggie eat' ... 'yes the doggie is eating'). Children whose parents expand or recast their speech do better on later tests of language ability (e.g., Vigil, Hodges & Klee, 2005).

Simple sentences

Three- to four-word sentences start to occur around the age of 24–27 months. These sentences may be grammatically incorrect but suggest that the child is using the rules of syntax (e.g., 'I pushed'/'I goed' or 'blocks gone away'/'mouses gone away'). Invented words are common (e.g., 'choskit', for chocolate biscuit) and grammatical rules are applied to these (choskit (s.) /choskits (pl.)). Once children have reached this stage there is a rapid increase in the use of grammatical rules, propositions and irregular verb endings. At this stage, children also begin to reorder words to produce questions and negatives, although initially they may not get these correct (e.g., 'where my shoe?', 'I no want it').

Children of this age also show great interest in rhymes and will spontaneously sing songs they have learned. Imaginative play gives the

Prelinguistic stages	0–12 months old ■ crying (from birth) ■ cooing (from 1 month) ■ babbling, echolalia (from 6–9 months)
Holophrastic (one-word) stage	Around 12–18 months old ■ first words appear ■ use of 'holophrases' ■ characteristic errors ■ increase in vocabulary
Telegraphic (two-word) stage	Around 18–24 months ■ emergence of simple two-word sentences ■ parents may expand or recast child's telegraphic speech
Simple sentences	Around 24–36 months ■ 3- or 4-word sentences ■ evidence for use of grammatical rules ■ interest in rhymes ■ idiosyncratic words ■ questions and negatives ■ monologues
3–5 years	■ larger vocabulary ■ longer sentences
Early school years	■ complex sentences ■ pragmatics
Middle childhood	■ refinements ■ exceptions to rules

Table 6.1 Universal stages in language development

opportunity to act out conversation or to give commentaries on activities. Children may talk to themselves before they go to sleep. These pre-sleep monologues may be important for processing interpersonal experiences and their subsequent organisation in memory. Weir (1962) recorded and analysed her child's bedtime monologues and concluded they serve three purposes: to practice newly acquired words and grammar, to play with sounds and to make sense of the world by ordering events in a systematic way.

Three–five years

From the age of three, the child's language is largely able to be understood by adults, even those outside the family. Vocabulary has increased to around 1,000 words, sentences are longer and the child is able to conduct reasonable conversations although these tend to be rooted in the present. Passive sentences which include mental states (e.g., was liked, was known) are particularly difficult but at this stage some types of passive are used.

Early school years

By the time child reaches school age his or her speech resembles that of an adult. Children are able to understand and to express complex sentences, and to adjust their speech to the level of the listener.

Middle childhood

This is a period of language refinement as the child learns exceptions to grammatical rules, as well as more complex syntactical structures. These refinements are gradual and may extend into adolescence (Uccelli et al., 2014).

Theories of language development

Whilst the method in which we develop language is thought to be largely universal, the way the rules of language are acquired is more contentious. There are two major approaches to syntactical development, one which emphasises the importance of the social environment in learning the rules and the other which supposes language is largely innate.

Empiricist account

This account is largely based around the principles proposed by learning approaches such as Skinner's operant conditioning model (1957), children learn language through selective reinforcement and imitation (Shaffer, Wood & Willoughby, 2002). Adults shape the speech of children reinforcing the babbling of infants that sound most like words. Correct utterances are positively reinforced when the child realises the communicative value of words and phrases. For example, if a child says 'milk', and he or she is then given milk, this enhances the child's language development (Ambridge & Lieven, 2011). Critics of the empiricist account highlight that learning through imitation and reinforcement would be a long and laboured process, whereas a child's language learning is a very fast process. Whilst children's language shows some imitation, there is also evidence of words and grammar the child has never heard. Children spontaneously learn the use of grammatical rules despite the fact that much of everyday speech is ungrammatical. Learning through imitation and reinforcement also fails to explain why children appear to have universal stages of language development. This theory also ignores the importance of biological factors in language development.

Nativist account

Noam Chomsky (1965) proposed the nativist account in which language is unique to humans. Chomsky claimed that all children had an innate language acquisition device (LAD), an area of the brain that has a set of universal syntactical rules. This device allows children to produce spontaneous and novel sentence based on their vocabulary. For example, according to this universal grammar account, children instinctively know how to combine a noun (e.g., 'a boy') and a verb ('to eat') into a meaningful sentence and correct phrase ('A boy eats'). They have an implicit knowledge of the rules of grammar such that they understand the order of words can change the meaning of the sentence ('The dog chased the cat' is different from 'The cat chased the dog'). His claims were based around the fact that children show an innate preference for language as infants attend to speech in preference to other sounds and that they master a complex system in a short space of time. They become effective speakers despite being exposed to ungrammatical speech and they will often put grammar into utterances when it is not needed. If children were to learn language purely through learning and imitation then their language would reflect these ungrammatical errors.

There is evidence to suggest that rather than copy sentences, children are able to abstract rules and create their own grammar, which they apply to new utterances that they have not heard before. Between the ages of two and seven they constantly adjust their grammar until it matches the adult population. There is thought to be a critical period in which to learn a first language, so that if a child does not hear language during this period, they will not be able to learn how to speak. The term 'critical period' of language was first established by Eric Lenneberg (1967). He proposed that there is one critical phase between the age of two and about 13 years (before puberty) in which an individual is able to acquire first language (FL). Acquiring a first language after this period is much more difficult and will never reach the level of language acquired during the critical period.

👁 Critical period and language acquisition

Language deprivation studies, also known as the forbidden experiments, have been attempted by isolating infants from the normal use of spoken and signed language. This has been done in an attempt to discover the fundamental character of human nature or the origin of language. For example, an alleged experiment carried out by the Roman Emperor Frederick II in the 13th century saw young infants collected from an orphanage and then brought up without human interaction in an attempt to determine if there was a natural language that they might demonstrate once their voices matured. Recorded in the chronicles of a monk named Salimbene di Adam, the story told is that children were allowed to be fed, nursed and washed by their foster mothers and nurses, but it was forbidden to talk to them. Frederick wanted to find out whether they would first speak Hebrew, Greek, Latin or Arabic. However, no child lived past their second birthday (Perry, 2002).

Such an experiment would not be able to be carried out today due the immorality of depriving a child from human interaction and communication. Yet there have been several cases in history where scientists were presented with children deprived of language, allowing them to address the idea of a critical period. One such case is that of Genie.

The case of Genie is one of the most infamous cases in history of a child reared in utter deprivation and isolation. Genie spent the first 13 years of her life imprisoned in a small room, often tied naked to a potty chair only able to move her hands and feet. When she made noises, her father would beat her and would often growl and bark at her. Her father, mother and older brother rarely spoke to her. As a result of her abuse, Genie did not acquire a first language. When she was found, a team of psychologists and language experts began the process of rehabilitating Genie (Curtiss, 1977). An important question was: could a child reared in utter deprivation and isolation develop language? Genie's case also presented researchers with a unique opportunity. If given an enriched learning environment, could she overcome her deprived childhood and learn language even though she had missed the critical period? If she could, it would suggest that the critical period hypothesis of language development was wrong. If she could not, it would indicate that Lenneberg's theory was correct.

Her rehabilitation team included graduate student Susan Curtiss and psychologist James Kent. Upon her initial arrival at UCLA, the team was met with a girl who weighed just 59 pounds and moved with a strange 'bunny walk'. She often spat and was unable to straighten her arms and legs. Silent, incontinent, and unable to chew, she initially seemed only able to recognise her own name and the word 'sorry'. After conducting an assessment of Genie's emotional and cognitive abilities, Kent described her as 'the most profoundly damaged child I've ever seen ... Genie's life is a wasteland'. Her silence and inability to use language made it difficult to assess her mental abilities, but on tests she scored at about the level of a one-year-old. She soon began to make rapid progression in specific areas, quickly learning how to use the toilet and dress herself. Over the next few months, she began to experience more developmental progress, but remained poor in some areas such as language. She enjoyed going out on day trips outside the hospital, and explored her new environment with an intensity that amazed her caregivers and strangers alike. Curtiss suggested that Genie had a strong ability to communicate nonverbally.

Despite scoring at the level of a one-year-old upon her initial assessment, Genie quickly began adding new words to her vocabulary. She started by learning single words and eventually began putting two words together much the way young children do. Curtiss began to feel that Genie would be fully capable of acquiring language. After a year of treatment, she even started putting three words together occasionally. In children going through normal language development, this stage is followed by what is known as a language explosion. Children rapidly acquire new words and begin putting them together in novel ways. Unfortunately, this never happened for Genie. Her language abilities remained stuck at this stage and she appeared unable to apply grammatical rules and use language in a meaningful way. At this point, her progress levelled off and her acquisition of new language halted. While Genie was able to learn some language after puberty, her inability to use grammar (which Chomsky suggests is what separates human language from animal communication) offers evidence for the critical period hypothesis. The critical period is usually defined as the maturational time period in which experience will have its peak effect on development of learning. Whilst the term 'critical period' is usually used in cases where there is an abrupt decline in the brain's plasticity, the term 'sensitive period' is thought to be more gradual. The terms are often used interchangeably (Newport, 1988). Genie was 13 years old when she was placed in a normal linguistic environment and therefore had passed the age of the critical time period to develop language. With increasing age of exposure to language there has been found a decline in average proficiency, beginning from the ages of four to six and stabilising in adulthood (Johnson & Newport, 1989).

Of course, Genie's case is not so simple. Not only did she miss the critical period for learning language, she was also horrifically abused. She also suffered abuse in one of her foster home placements. She was malnourished and deprived of cognitive stimulation for most of her childhood. Researchers were also never able to fully determine if Genie suffered from pre-existing cognitive deficits. As an infant, a paediatrician had identified her as having some type of mental delay. However extreme deprivation has been shown to lead to poorer development of brain regions (Bremner, 1999).

Another similar case is that of Victor of Aveyron. In 1799, some peasants in Tarn and Aveyron, in southern France, encountered a naked 12-year-old boy scavenging alone in the forests. He did not speak and seemed not to understand speech, as the only noises he could produce were grunts and whines. He was known to the mountain farmers as a boy who moved unusually quickly on four limbs. The boy must have survived alone in the wild for many years, living off acorns and small animals he could scavenge in the forests (McCrone, 1993). He was eventually captured and transferred to the institute of deaf mutes in Paris. The first team working with the boy, now named Victor, concluded that he was either 'insane' or 'an idiot' and gave up trying to teach him to speak. However he was eventually passed in the care of a physician called Jean-Marc Gaspard Itard who worked with him daily for two years. Itard tried to teach Victor to speak through a combination of food rewards and physical punishment. In 1806, Itard gave up and although Victor had learnt some basic signs critically he never learnt to speak.

◉ Interactionist theory

Interactionist theories stress the importance of both biological factors and social interactions in the development of language. Interactionists argue that 'children are born with a powerful brain that matures slowly, and predispose them to acquire new understandings that they are motivated to share with others' (Bates, 1993; Tomasello, 1993; as cited in Shaffer, Wood & Willoughby, 2002, p. 362).

Evidence to support interactionist views has stemmed from studies in three key areas.

Relationship between language and cognition: For example, Piaget's theory on children learning language is mainly focused around cognitive development. If a baby uses sentences involving phrases such as 'more than' and 'less than' it means the concepts of 'more than' have been achieved before they are able to use it in a sentence.

Language and social interaction: As a response to Chomsky's LAD system, Bruner (1983) put forward the Language Acquisition Support System (LASS). Bruner states through the LASS that parents use books and images to develop children's naming abilities and to get involved in conversation as an interactive process.

Adult–child speech: Caregivers unconsciously modify their speech when talking to infants and toddlers. The modified speech is typified by such things as the adult speaking in monologues, using grammatically simple structures and using exaggerated intonation. In the first year of a child's life caregivers largely use long segments of talk (monologues), with little involvement from the child other than attention. When the child reaches about 18 months, caregivers tend to address the child in a more grammatically simple manner with topics restricted to the here-and-now, such as what a child is currently doing. Then when the child reaches about age two, caregivers tend to repeat words and phrases, often in an exaggerated tone with a higher pitch.

Recent studies have argued that child-directed speech makes language acquisition easier for infants (Thiessen, Hill & Saffran, 2005). However, children's whose parents do not use child-directed speech have been found to learn language just as well. Equally, whilst various studies have found child-directed speech in speakers of English, German, Russian, Swedish and Mandarin Chinese, there are many cultures that do not use any (Schieffelin & Ochs, 1987). It is also important to note that much language learning occurs through children simply listening to adults conversing.

Summary

- Neither learning or nativist approaches offer a complete account, although both may be partially correct
- Biological maturation affects cognitive development and this in turn influences language development
- Importance of the social environment

Chapter 7

Emotional Development

Understanding a child's emotional development helps to make sense of a child's behaviour. It will help to think about, and acknowledge how the child might be feeling at a particular time and enable one to help him/her to work through what has been experienced. It is important to remember that each child develops in his or her own unique way depending on personality, and that children *develop at different rates.*

Emotional development

Emotion, the ability to think and feel is a complex and subjective experience involving both biological and behavioural changes. Human emotions are considered to have four components. Importantly, there is no clear agreement as to whether all four components occur for every emotional event.

Cognitive reactions: Perception, thinking and memory involved in emotional expression.

Affect: A valence experience related to a positive or negative state.

Physiological reactions: Physical changes in the body, from levels in hormones and heart rate, to blushing.

In this chapter, we will examine:
- What are 'emotions'?
- At what age do children first show emotions?
- What is their significance in child development? And does that change over time?

Behavioural responses: Emotions change us and prepare us to react and actively express our feelings and emotional states.

There has been much debate as to the specific function of emotions. The clearest explanation of function has stemmed from the evolutionary perspective, which suggests that emotions have three primary functions: adaptation and survival, as they alert us to danger and contamination; regulation, as the changes we experience affect how we perceive things and events in the world; and communication, as they transmit our feelings and needs to others (Roberts, 2003).

The first evolutionary account came from Charles Darwin in the 1870s, who proposed that emotions evolved because they have an adaptive value. For example, the emotion of fear exists to enhance one's chances of survival. Darwin also believed that we have innate facial expressions of emotion, which have evolved to communicate our intentions to, and understand the intentions of, others. In 1868, he undertook a study to prove that humans, like animals, have an innate and universal set of emotional expressions, a code through which we understand others' feelings. The experiment started in his house in Kent, whereby he asked guests during a series of dinner parties, for their responses to black and white photographs of a man with his face frozen into a range of different positions. This was followed by a questionnaire that was distributed around the world, one of the first questionnaires ever invented. According to his notes, his subjects unanimously agreed on certain photographs – those that portrayed fear, surprise, happiness, sadness and anger. In his book *The Expression of Emotion in Man and Animals*, he outlined his view that expression was shared amongst humans and animals.

Since then, many theorists have tried to explain why and how people feel different emotions. In the 1890s, the psychologist William Lange put forward what is now known as the James–Lange theory. The idea was that people experience emotion because they perceive physiological changes in their bodies as responses to external events. This theory implies that people cry not because they feel sad but instead they feel sad because they cry or they feel happy because they smile. Despite being able to explain the different physiological reactions associated with different emotions, this account has been heavily refuted. A physiologist, Walter Cannon, was one of the leading critics of this theory highlighting that physiological reactions happen too slowly to cause the actual emotion, and that often people experience very different emotions even when they have the same pattern of physiological arousal. For example, a racing heart and rapid breathing can occur when a person is both angry and afraid. In the 1920s Cannon proposed his own theory, which was expanded by Philip Bard in the 1930s so it is named the Cannon–Bard theory. This theory acknowledges that whilst the experience of emotion co-occurs with the physiological arousal, neither one causes the other. The main argument of their theory is that experience of emotion and physiological arousal occur simultaneously, the brain gets the message that causes the experience of the emotion as the autonomic nervous system gets the message that causes the physiological reaction. Therefore, if someone is afraid of heights and is travelling up a skyscraper, they will experience fear. However, critics argue that not all people will have the same emotion despite having the same physiological reaction. The Schacter–Singer theory (1962) suggests emotions have two factors; physiological arousal and cognition (understanding of arousal). It is these cognitions that are used to interpret meaning of physiological reactions. Some recent theories of emotion have built on the Schacter–Singer theory, and feature one's **cognitive appraisal** of emotion. For example, people's experience of emotion depends on the way they appraise or evaluate events around them (Lazarus, 1991b).

The most popular and widely accepted view today is that emotions are innate. Through extensive international studies, Paul Ekman has shown that facial expressions of emotion are not culturally determined, but are universal across human cultures. Expressions he found to be universal included anger, disgust, fear, joy, sadness and surprise. Another psychologist, Carroll Izard (2009), also argued that emotions are innate and that they are discrete from one another from a very early age (two to seven months), and each emotion is believed to show specific and distinctive set of bodily and facial reactions.

Summary

- Emotional responses comprise four main aspects: cognitive reaction, affect, physiological reactions and behavioural reactions.
- Emotions may serve several purposes: promotion of survival (avoiding danger/harm); regulation; promotion of communication.
- Cross-cultural and comparative studies confirm that the facial expressions associated with several 'basic' emotions are recognised universally and may be innate.

👁 Development of emotions

From birth babies start signalling their emotional states. The earliest distinction one can make is between positive and negative affect and this occurs during the first two months of life. Emotions that occur in the first two years have been called fundamental or primary emotions (Lewis & Michalson, 1983). These emotions are characterised both by early appearance and by having prototypical and universal facial expressions for each. It is generally agreed that babies experience six primary emotions: joy, fear, anger, surprise, sadness and disgust.

Happiness

Happiness can be seen during the early weeks of life and is expressed with joyful smiles resulting from affection and stimulation from caregivers and through gentle touches and sounds. The baby will also smile upon achieving new skills. Social interaction usually begins around three months of age and laughter at around three to four months. It is not until six months when the baby smiles and laughs more on contact with familiar people. Around 10–12 months, babies will show several differentiating smiles depending on the context. A broad smile from cheek to cheek is awarded to parents, a reserved smile to a friendly stranger and mouth open smile when engaged in play. By two years the smile displayed is intentional.

Anger and sadness

Anger occurs when the infant is hungry or needs changing. The intensity of anger increases from four months up to two years and more commonly occurs when an expected outcome does not occur (Mireault & Trahan, 2007). Anger is commonly expressed in an assortment of behaviour including hitting, kicking, crying and screaming. Sadness can also result from similar contexts as anger, and young children express this emotion with similar behaviours. It tends to be expressed less frequently than anger.

Fear

Fear begins around six months of age and can be associated with being left alone, meeting strangers and sudden loud noises. Rise in fear can come as a hurdle to children as they begin their exploratory behaviour of crawling and walking. It is also around seven months when an infant shows a fear of strangers. In the first few months of life they usually seem interested in both familiar adults as well as strangers engaging in such games as peek-a-boo. However, at six months they will begin a process of fearing strangers and will react strongly if someone unfamiliar to them tries to make eye contact, hold them or if they are left alone with them (Stevenson-Hinde & Shouldice, 2013).

Stranger anxiety and separation anxiety both develop around eight to nine months. They form a normal part of a child's cognitive development. The infant is now able to differentiate their caregivers and shows strong preferences for them. They will react more strongly to people that look very different to their caregivers, for example someone wearing glasses or having a beard. The degree of distress shown by an infant towards strangers or being separated from their caregiver will vary greatly depending on the temperament of the individual child (Brooker et al., 2013).

Disgust

Disgust is also recognised as a universal emotion. It's expression is demonstrated by characteristic facial features of wrinkling the upper nose and raising the upper lip, thereby wrinkling the lower nose (Ekman & Friesen, 1978). The primary function of disgust is protection against contaminated entities and quite often it relates to a reaction to food, with the facial expressions communicating smelling something unpleasant or which tastes bad. Izard (1994) suggested that young children will often use caregivers' facial expressions to learn what is disgusting and therefore disgust provides a child a way in which to recognise disgust in others. Whilst considered a basic emotion, there is some evidence to suggest children are poor at recognising the emotion in others, often confusing the open mouth with the expression of anger.

Summary

- Primary emotions refer to some 'basic' emotions which are discernible from the first few weeks onwards. They are happiness, surprise, sadness, fear, disgust and anger (Table 7.1).
- Fear can occur in periods of separation.
- Fear responses increase after seven months.
- Anger and fear become distinguished from each other after seven months.

Babies 0–1 months	Crying is normal mode of expression. ■ Needs to feel calm and safe
2–3 months	Beginning to communicate by showing a variety of feelings and expressing emotions through smiles, frowns, body movements, gurgling and cooing. ■ Is soothed through close contact and food ■ Recognises familiar people and will respond to them with smiles
4–6 months	Starting to fear strangers/people unfamiliar to them. ■ Able to show happiness through smiles ■ Reassured when in contact with familiar people and when cuddled
6–12 months	Develops clinging to parents behaviour ■ Will show resistant behaviours if not happy ■ Enjoys attention ■ Comforts him/herself with a familiar toy or thumb sucking ■ Fear and sadness are now openly expressed by the child
12–24 months	Beginning to show negative emotions and may resist naps, refuse some foods and may have tantrums ■ Begins to understand turn-taking games ■ Needs comfort and reassurance from parents/carers ■ Afraid of being apart from carer can cause distress when separated
Two years	Shows extreme behaviour – dependent/interdependent, very aggressive/calm, and helpful/stubborn. ■ Temper tantrums are common and tends to cry, scream, kick, bite and can be rough with other children ■ Reliant on parent/teacher to distinguish right from wrong ■ Limited ability to attend to things for long periods of time ■ Has little concept of sharing ■ Needs routine and becomes upset when changes occur ■ More complex emotions develop such as sympathy and pride. increased awareness of praise and approval ■ Becoming more independent ■ Fear develops for certain loud noises (trains, thunder) ■ Fear of strangers decreases

Table 7.1 Stages of emotional development in early childhood

👁 Self-conscious emotions

Whilst primary emotions such as fear, anger and joy emerge in the first year of life, it is not until the second half of the second year of life that the earliest of the self-conscious emotions present themselves.

Self-conscious emotions develop at the same time a child develops self-reflection/awareness – or what Lewis has called 'consciousness', the mental representation of 'me' (Lewis, 2000). These secondary emotions depend on a baby's new abilities to be aware of, talk about, and think about themselves in relation to other people. Secondary emotions are also called social emotions (Barrett, 1995) and 'self-conscious' emotions (Lewis, 2007).

Self-recognition during early childhood is often indexed by the emergence of the mirror self-recognition (MSR) or the rouge test (Lewis & Brooks-Gunn, 1979). In the typical MSR task, an experimenter surreptitiously places a mark on the child's head and then the child is allowed to look in the mirror. If the child attempts to remove the mark from his/her own head, he/she is said to have self-recognition. If, however, the child points to or reaches for the mirror image he/she has not. Children do not usually pass until 18–24 months of age (Figure 7.1).

The earliest self-conscious emotions, in the order they develop, include embarrassment, jealousy, empathy as well as shame, guilt, pride and envy. These emotions require the cognitive ability to reflect on the self but often without the understanding of rules and standards and goals of the people around them and develop around 15–24 months (Lewis,

Figure 7.1 Example of Rouge test

2003). Embarrassment first occurs when a child develops the idea of 'me' and begins to understand that they become the object of another person's attentions. Empathy also emerges as the child is now able to place themselves in the role of others, and by understanding the role of others the emotion jealousy also occurs (Figure 7.2).

It is not until the third year of a child's life that emotions attached to the rules, standards and goals of others (friends, family and their peers) start to occur. These emotions, guilt, shame and pride, are considered to have evaluative components as the child's emotions are regulated by others' expectations.

Shame is complex and results when a child evaluates their own behaviour as failing to meet the goals and standards of others as well as their own goals. It is a very negative emotion resulting in disruption of a child's on-going behaviour and is associated with the child's desire to disappear or hide (Lewis, 1997). The emotion of guilt is similar, in the sense that the child will evaluate a failure to meet other's expectations, but the focus is shifted to either very specific aspects of self and/or their actions that led to that failure in order to repair the damage. The emotion of guilt tends to be less negative than that of shame, as the focus tends to be on attributions and also what they are able do to fix the action (Bafunno & Camodeca, 2013).

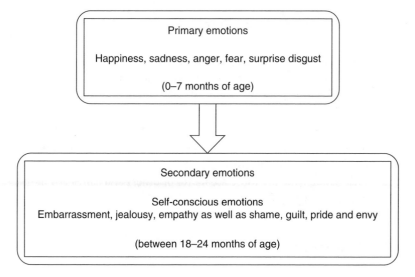

Figure 7.2 Primary and secondary emotions

The emotions of envy and jealousy are sometimes considered together as if they were the same. However, some authors (e.g., Lazarus, 1991a) differentiate between them. Envy is usually associated with physical belongings that the child wants, whereas jealousy usually involves a third person.

The final self-conscious emotion to be considered is the extremely dislikeable hubris, associated with both grandiosity and narcissism (Morrison, 1989). Hubris tends to be defined an exaggerated pride or self-confidence where the success at one's standards, rule and goals is focused entirely on the self with little consideration of others. Children who receive unnecessary praise and are praised too regularly are in danger of developing hubris (Mueller & Dweck, 1998). Prideful people have difficulty in their interpersonal relations due to an inability to ignore their own wishes and desires and these come at the consequences of those of others often resulting in interpersonal conflict (Lewis, 2000).

We move from basic emotions to those where socialisation plays an increasing role in determining what situation will elicit what emotions. The cultural rules and a child's individual temperament also play a role in how emotions develop. However, the evaluative self-conscious emotions, also considered moral emotions, truly set us apart from the rest of the animal world.

Relationship between sense of self, and understanding of others

When the sense of self develops, around 18 months or so, our understanding of others develops too. Lewis and Brooks-Gunn (1979) advanced three principles that come with development of self:

1 Any knowledge about the other may be gained about the self.
2 What can be demonstrated to be known about the self can be said to be known about the other.
3 Social dimension are those attributes of others and self that can be used to describe people.

Empathy

Emotional development (having feelings), how we understand our own and others development, and to develop our ability to 'stand in someone else's shoes' is often referred to as empathy. Early theorists suggested that young children were too egocentric or otherwise not cognitively able to experience empathy (Freud, 1958; Piaget, 1932). However, recent studies have consistently shown that young children are, in fact, capable of displaying a variety of empathy-related behaviours. One typical way of measuring empathy in young children is to examine their responses to another's distress.

As early as 18–72 hours following birth, newborns have been shown to respond more strongly to another infant's cry than to a variety of control stimuli, including silence, non-human cry sounds and even their own cry (Martin & Clark, 1982). This phenomenon of infants showing distress responses to the sound of another infant crying has been referred to as reflexive crying or emotional contagion. The specificity of only responding to another infant crying, suggests that there may be a biological predisposition for humans to respond to the negative emotion of others. Feelings of personal distress in response to others' negative emotional experience during infancy are thought to be the precursor to empathic concern. This is largely due to the fact that young children are unable to differentiate the self from others.

Empathy in the first two years of life is then based around:

- Personal distress of other's emotional reaction.
- 'Emotional contagion' where the child displays the same emotion to the other person.
- 'Egocentric empathy' where the child endeavours to comfort by offering kinds of help they find comforting.

The capability for concern for another has been found to develop alongside the self–other differentiation, perspective-taking and emotion regulation during the second year of life. For example, at 18 months infants have been shown to 'watch' or 'ignore' sibling distress if unrelated to their own actions. But at 36 months are more likely to offer comfort. Children are able to recognise the expressions of siblings and respond in ways which serve to modify their sibling's emotional state. They modify their response according to circumstances.

Zahn-Waxler and colleagues have carried out vast numbers of studies looking at empathy-related behaviours in the second and third years of life. In a series of studies with children aged 14–36 months they examined children's responses to the simulated distress of a stranger and of their parent, at home and in the laboratory. Amongst their empathy measures, included concern (e.g., looking sad, saying 'I'm sorry'), hypothesis testing (e.g., asking 'What happened?'), prosocial behaviour (e.g., hugging and/or asking 'Are you ok?') as well as precursors to empathy such as personal distress and self-referential behaviours. All empathic behaviours were found to increase between 14–24 years of age and all children engaged in some form of helping behaviours by the time they were two years old (Knafo, Zahn-Waxler, Van Hulle, Robinson & Rhee, 2008). The quality of prosocial behaviour also increases during the second year of life. The youngest children were found to rely on physical responses, by 18–20 months toddlers could use verbal comfort and advice, and by their third year children could express concern verbally and through facial expression and exhibited a wider variety of helping behaviours (Zahn-Waxler, Radke-Yarrow, Wagner & Chapman, 1992).

Empathy has both emotional and cognitive components which can be experienced separately. Emotional empathy is the sharing the experience of another's emotion state which appears even in newborns. In contrast, cognitive empathy, sometimes referred to as 'theory of mind' (ToM) or perspective-taking, is the ability to accurately imagine another's experience (Saxe, 2006). Cognitive empathy improves considerably as children enter and progress through primary school.

The ability to reflect on one's emotions and the emotions of others has been termed **theory of mind**. It reflects one's ability to infer the full range of mental states (beliefs, desires, intentions, emotions, etc.) that underlie people's behaviour. Children at around four–five years of age have been shown to be capable of taking another's perspective in **'false belief' tasks**, an common test used to indicate development of theory of mind. Wimmer and Perner (1983) proposed one of the first false belief tasks. They told a story to four-year-old subjects about Maxi, who put some chocolate in a blue cupboard. Maxi left the room and while he was out of the room Maxi's mother moved the chocolate into the green cupboard. The four-year-olds were asked to predict where Maxi would look for the chocolate. If a child had a theory of mind they would respond with the original location (blue cupboard) rather than the true location (green cupboard). Children with a developed theory of mind understand that Maxi doesn't know the true location, even though they themselves do. The ability to understand other's perspectives is integral for fully and successfully identifying with another's experience which also allows a child to engage in more effective helping strategies (Figure 7.3).

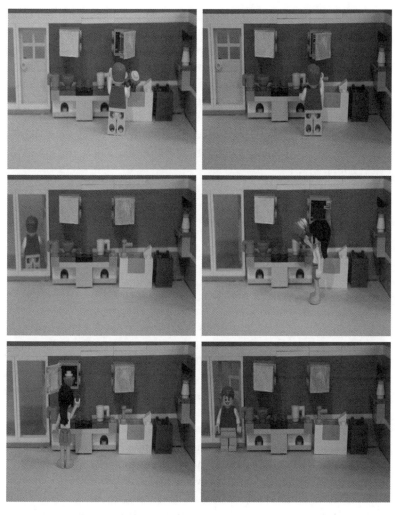

Figure 7.3 The Maxi-task test presented using toys

Not all children are as empathic as each other. What affects empathy development? Knafo and colleagues (2008) carried out a study to investigate the relative contributions of genetics and shared environment. In their study, young children's responses to simulated distress were measured in monozygotic (identical) and dizygotic (fraternal) twins at 14, 20, 24 and 36 months of age. By 24 to 36 months of age heritability was associated with one-third to almost one-half of the variation in children's empathy. In other words, nearly two-thirds to a half of a child's potential for empathic development *may* be due to their environmental experiences. Parental warmth has also been found to be important in promoting empathy. Toddlers and children who have parents who were observed to display more warmth towards them during a variety of inter-actions tended to be more empathic (Zhou et al., 2002). Young children who have close relationships to older siblings have also been shown to be more empathic (Tucker, Updegraff, McHale & Crouter, 1999). Tempera-ment has also been found to affect empathy, with shy preschool children rated higher in both empathy and guilt than other children (Cornell & Frick, 2007).

Summary

- Precursors to empathic responses are seen in newborns
- Development of empathy appears to follow development of self–other differentiation
- Parental behaviour and child's temperament affect empathy development

Socialisation and communication

The term 'social referencing' is used to describe the moments when babies learn how they should react to unfamiliar objects, people or events by carefully watching their caregivers' reactions to these things. The carer becomes the 'reference' as the infant uses the carer's emotional expression to determine how to react to a situation. Most parents will smile and encourage their babies when in a safe environment such as playing with a new toy, but will react by pulling their child away and showing fear in aversive situations such as unfamiliar animals. By using the caregiver's cues (such as facial expressions, body language and tone of voice), the child learns what is considered dangerous and to be avoided (Vaish & Striano, 2004). Research has shown that by 12 months of age, babies use visual information from the faces of caregivers to make sense of situations that are new or unclear. Scientists have also found that caregivers' negative reactions seem to make a more powerful impact on babies than positive ones. This makes sense in that we are more likely to react quickly and dramatically when a baby, for example, reaches for an open oven door given that it is very important that the baby learns not to touch that door.

Social referencing ability has been demonstrated in various paradigms in which infants are placed in novel, ambiguous situations about which an adult expresses some affect, such as happiness or fear. The infant's behaviour towards the situation is then assessed in order to examine whether or not the adult's affect influenced the infants. One of the most common ways to examine social referencing is to use the 'visual cliff' (Gibson & Walk, 1960). The visual cliff involves a table with a deep cliff on half of it but covered with a transparent glass. The child is positioned on one side and invited by the mother to crawl over the cliff, over the glass. In the classic study using this paradigm, Sorce, Emde, Campos and Klinnert (1985) found that infants cross over to the deep side of the visual cliff if their mother poses a positive facial expression but not if she poses a negative one. When depth cues are removed from the visual cliff, infants tend to not even look at their mother, and if they do look, not to guide their behaviour as a function of her facial expression. Importantly, infants manifest similar skills when they encounter novel objects or toys (Klinnert, 1984) and when responding to strangers. Feiring, Lewis and Starr (1984) observed how babies aged 15 months responded to a stranger and found that the infants' reactions mirrored that of their mothers (Figure 7.4).

Figure 7.4 Visual cliff test

Summary

- Early capacities for emotion expression and recognition are the foundation of communication and social learning.
- Infants learn appropriate emotional reactions to events and people through social referencing.
- A baby's behaviours and their emotional reactions are also regulated through the reactions of their caregivers.

Theory of mind

Crucially important in a child's emotional development is the ability of a child to understand the feelings, thoughts and perspective of others (ToM). It is generally assumed that children develop theory of mind as an understanding of others around the age of four. The 'Sally–Ann task' (Baron-Cohen, Leslie & Frith 1985) is seen as a less complex task compared to the Maxi task described above, and children could perform it correctly at slightly earlier age. In this version, 'Sally' puts a marble in her basket and then leaves. While she is absent 'Ann' takes the marble form the basket and outs it in her own box. Sally returns and the children are asked, 'Where will Sally look for her marble?' Four-year-olds typically choose the basket and three-year-olds typically the box. A even simpler version of this theory of mind task was created to rule out the possibility that younger children were failing the task due to story incomprehension. In the 'Smartie task' (Perner, Leekam & Wimmer, 1987) children were shown a tube of Smarties (a common UK brand of sweet or candy) and asked what they thought was in the tube. They were then shown that rather than there being sweets in the tube, like most of the children predicted, there were pencils. They were then asked what a person who had *not* seen inside the tube would think was in the tube? Only children of four years correctly predicted that the person would also predict sweets. Results of theory of mind tasks usually suggest that before the age of four years, children have difficulty understanding that another person can have a false belief about the world. However research has shown that even at the age of two, children show some understanding of others.

Distinguishing mental stages in language

Around two, children use the words 'look', 'see' and 'taste' and by three years use cognitive terms like 'know', 'think' and 'remember'. Shatz and colleagues (1983) found that three-year-olds could distinguish between mental states and external reality. In another study, Wellman and Estes (1986) showed three-year-olds two story characters, and the children were told that character A had a biscuit and actor B was thinking about a biscuit. Children asked which of the two (physical and mental) biscuits could be touched or seen by another character. Three-year-olds could accurately make the distinction between physical and mental states.

Understanding the relationship between seeing and knowing

From two years children show understanding between seeing and knowing. Lempers, Flavell & Flavell (1977) asked two-year-olds to show another person a picture glued to a corner in a box. Children had to realise that the box needed to be shown at a certain angle for others to see it; also those who had hands over their eyes would not be able to see it. Three-year-olds understand that different people may have different views of same object, Masangkay and colleagues (1974) used a card with a cat drawn on one side and a dog on the other. It was held upright with one side facing child and the other the experimenter. Three-year-olds understood that the experimenter saw a different picture to them, showing that children can appreciate that people can have different perspectives. However, it is not until four years of age that children realise that others have different views on an object. Masangkay and colleagues (1974) tested children aged three to five years. The children were shown a picture of an upright turtle; it appeared to be standing on its feet if it was the 'right' way up and when 'upside down' it appeared as if on its back. With the picture placed flat on a table between the child and the experimenter sitting at opposite sides of table, all children could describe their own view but only a one-third of three-year-olds could describe the experimenter's view.

False belief

Experiments have shown that about four years of age children realise that another person can have inaccurate beliefs about the world. The false belief task involves a 'first order' belief ('I think that Sally thinks that the marble is in the basket'). A 'second order belief' is one that involves understanding a third person's belief ('I think that Jack thinks that Jill thinks that the marble is the basket'). Perner and Wimmer (1985) designed a task to test this process. John and Mary are playing in the park and spot an ice cream van. Mary goes home to get some money to get an ice cream, whilst John goes home for lunch. On the way back Mary sees the ice cream van moving and follows it to school. In the meantime, John goes to Mary's house and he is told that Mary has gone to get an ice cream. Children are then asked 'Where does John think that Mary went to buy an ice cream?' Children typically succeed at this task at around six years of age.

Deception

Deception involves altering the belief of others. Peskin (1992) carried out an experiment with children aged three, four and five years. Children are shown stickers and told to pick their favourite one. They are then told two puppets could come, one would be nice and if it is shown their favourite sticker it would not take it; the other puppet, a 'nasty' puppet, would take their favourite sticker. All children showed their favourite sticker to the nice puppet. However, for the nasty puppet, the five-year-olds realised they could manipulate its beliefs (generate a false belief) and pointed to the sticker they did not want. By the fourth trial of the experiment the four-year-olds learnt to do the same, but the three-year-olds continually showed their favourite sticker.

Emotional deception

Based on theory of mind we see that children begin to manipulate emotions around the ages of three or four. Cole (1986) looked at how three- and four-year-old girls would react when given a disappointing present. Four-year-old girls were more likely to mask their disappointment. In other studies with children of similar age, children have been shown to display more positive affect when their mother was present than when their mother was absent, showing their awareness of how their mother might expect them to behave. However children who are younger than four years of age are not very good at being able to mask their true feelings. For example, Lewis and colleagues (1989) told children that they were going to put a surprise on the table but they were not allowed to look. Children who peeked tended to put on a smile when the experimenter re-entered the room.

◉ Understanding others' emotions, desires and beliefs

Beginnings of understanding others' emotions, desires and beliefs are seen at two years. There are important precursors or preconditions to understanding another person's mind. Two-year-olds have a 'theory' based on 'desire psychology'. They assume that people's desires influence their behaviour. For example, Sam wants to take his rabbit to school but cannot find it. Children will understand that Sam will continue looking for his rabbit so he can take it to school. By three, children have a theory that takes into account a person's desire, but also beliefs about the world. Bartsch and Wellman (1995) more recently concluded that three-year-olds have some awareness of other people's minds but still act very much based on desire psychology.

Perner (1991) has argued that understanding minds comes when children can understand false belief. This occurs when children have required the 'metarepresentation' distinction between what is referred to and what is represented. For example, a photo of a pyramid taken from the ground looks like a triangle, whereas if taken from above it looks like a square. So when a four-year-old succeeds on a false belief task like the Maxi task, the child can make the distinction between *what* is represented (chocolate in location A) and *how* it is represented (by Maxi, chocolate in location B). Leslie and Frith (1987) uses 'metarepresentation' to describe pretend play, as children can show pretend play from 18 months. Young children are quite happy to pretend that a banana is a telephone and do not get confused and call all telephones 'bananas'. Children must have two representations (thinking about a banana as a banana) and a secondary representation (metarepresentation). Children's ability to coordinate play with others implies they understand what is in the mind of the children they are playing with.

Harris (1989) argues that children can understand others' minds without necessarily understanding that others have mental representational abilities. Instead children use 'simulations'. Here, children can project emotions and explanations of emotions onto others. So a child faced with the Sally–Ann task could imagine what she herself would think and do if she was Sally, and then work out what actions and consequences would follow. It is only by the age of four that children realise that different people may have different attitudes towards the same objects and can take into account alternative views. This involves reasoning about situations that are counter to reality ('counterfactual' information).

Counterfactual reasoning was emphasised by Riggs and colleagues (1998), here three- and four-year-olds were tested using a modified version of the Maxi task. This included an additional part of the story where Maxi's mother uses the chocolate to make a cake rather than simply moving it to another location. This additional component to the story allowed a counterfactual element to be tested. Children were asked two questions about the story: 'Where does Maxi think the chocolate is?' The correct answer assumed to be based on mental representations. The other question 'If mum had not made a cake, where would the chocolate be?' which relies on hypothetical reasoning. Nearly all children who answered the false belief question correctly answered the reasoning question correctly, and nearly all the children who failed the false belief question also failed the reasoning question.

These theories of cognitive development can apply to emotions. For example, theory of mind provides a starting point for assessing how far children have come in understanding the emotions of others. Pretend play is important for perspective-taking and imaginative understanding.

Summary

- Understanding others' emotions, desires and beliefs begins around two years old.
- At about four years old, children develop ToM and realise that another person can have inaccurate beliefs about the world.
- ToM development can be assessed using false belief tasks involving 'first order' and 'second order' beliefs.
- Desire psychology, metarepresentation and counterfactual reasoning have all been offered as explanations for why children may pass or fail ToM tests.

Emotion and gender

A common stereotype exists that girls are more emotional than boys (Fischer, 1993). The ability to recognise emotions quickly and accurately is an important social skill. We know that children's recognition of the basic emotions (happy, sad, angry, fear, surprise, disgust) develops quite early (around five years old) and is as good as adults by around 10–12 years old. However research has shown mixed findings in regards to whether females show better emotion *recognition* than males. Gender differences in children's emotion *expression* have been observed as early as the preschool years, with girls being less likely to show anger, and more likely to show sadness, than boys (Brody, 1999). One source of influence on such gender differences may be the socialisation pressures that orient girls and boys toward different roles in life (Brody & Hall, 2000). These socialisation pressures, may not always be obvious or overt (e.g., 'big boys do not cry') but may be subtle, conveyed in the form of differential attention to boys' and girls' expressions during emotional events, attention that may subtly encourage the expression of certain emotions and discourage others (Fivush & Buckner, 2000). This may contribute to a tendency for girls to be more likely than boys to convey submissive emotions, such as sadness and anxiety, and for boys to be more willing to express disharmonious emotions, such as anger and laughing at another (Brody, 2000).

One possibility is that parents socialise their children to express gender role-consistent emotions through parenting practices of which they are consciously aware (Eisenberg, Cumberland & Spinrad, 1998). Empirical support for this hypothesis is mixed. Some studies find that parents report being more accepting of girls' sadness and anxiety, and of boys' anger (Casey & Fuller, 1994; Eisenberg, Fabes & Murphy, 1996), but other studies fail to reveal gender-differentiated patterns in parents' self-reported reactions to children's emotions (Eisenberg & Fabes, 1994). Malatesta and Haviland (1982) found gender differences in mothers' responses to infant emotion, with mothers attending more to boys' happiness and matching sons' emotions more than their daughters'. Interestingly, Malatesta and Haviland did not find gender differences in how mothers verbally encouraged or discouraged the emotion. Dunn and colleagues (1987) found mothers talked more about feelings with girls than boys; and Saarni (1984) found girls more likely than boys to mask feelings of disappointment. In summary, these findings suggest that overall attention given to a child's emotion is an important feature of emotion socialisation.

◉ Moral emotions

Moral emotions represent an important but often overlooked element of our human moral apparatus. Moral emotions may be critically important in understanding people's behavioural adherence (or lack of adherence) to their moral standards. Haidt (2003) defines moral emotions as those 'that are linked to the interests or welfare either of society as a whole or at least of persons other than the judge or agent' (p. 276). Moral emotions are the motivators behind acting good and avoiding doing something bad

(Kroll & Egan, 2004). Shame, guilt, embarrassment and pride are all classed as members of the 'self-conscious emotions' family, being induced by both self-reflection and self-evaluation. This self-evaluation may not necessarily be at the conscious level. As the self reflects upon the self, moral self-conscious emotions provide instant punishment (or reinforcement) of behaviour. These self-conscious emotions provide us a measure for whether our behaviour is socially acceptable (Tangney, Stuewig & Mashek, 2007).

Chapter 8

Moral Development

Moral reasoning also known as moral judgement refers to how we reason, or judge, whether an action is right or wrong. How children learn this important skill and use this knowledge to decide how to act when faced with difficult choices is part of moral development. Children learn the moral rules which govern their behaviour and to act in accordance with the right decision, even when it may not be the most convenient thing to do.

As with other components of development, morality is shaped by multiple factors. Children's experiences at home, the environment around them, and their physical, cognitive, emotional and social skills are thought all to influence their developing sense of right vs wrong. However, the age at which a child becomes morally responsible is heavily debated. This question has becomes particularly salient in recent years with public moral debate over the culpability of children who commit violent crimes.

In this chapter, we will examine:
- Definitions of morality and its importance in development
- The key theorists of moral development: Piaget, Kolhberg and Eisenberg
- Moral emotions
- Influence on later development
- Nature vs nurture
- Cultural and gender differences

Morality is a sense of behavioural conduct that differentiates intentions, decisions and actions between those that are good (or right) and bad (or wrong). Morality is typically an intuitive reaction, but is famously linked to cognition. We begin this chapter with two main cognitive developmental theories.

Piaget's moral development theory

Jean Piaget (1932) was one of the first psychologists to put forward a theory as to how children learn morals, and much of his work still remains relevant today. His early ideas focused on how children learn right or wrong in the context of game playing. According to Piaget, development emerges from action, so that children construct their knowledge as a result of their interactions with others and the environment. Based on his observations of rules when playing a game, Piaget proposed that morality was also a developmental process.

In his book *The Moral Development of the Child* (1932), Piaget reported his studies in which he observed children playing the game of marbles. Piaget would watch children of different ages (between 3 and 12) and get them to explain to him the rules and the reasons for the rules. Piaget pretended to be ignorant of the rules of the game. He was thus able to investigate the way that children themselves understood the rules, and to observe how children of different ages related to the rules and the game. Piaget believed that the understanding and application of rules can explain how people relate to each other. The game of marbles was ideal for Piaget as children normally played it without adult supervision or interference.

Piaget also studied the way children understand and use rules by using short stories with different degrees of bad outcomes and situations, asking children to explain who they thought was guilty and why, and also to elaborate on the possible punishment deserved for the action. Typically Piaget would compare pairs of stories. For example:

> *A little boy called John was in his room. He was called to dinner and went into the dining room. Behind the door there was a chair and on the chair there was a tray with 15 cups on it. John couldn't have known that the chair was behind the door, and as he entered the dining room, the door knocked against the tray and the tray fell on the floor, breaking all of the cups.*

One day, a little boy called Henry tried to get some jam out of a cupboard when his mother was out. He climbed onto a chair and stretched out his arm. The jam was too high up, and he couldn't reach it. But while he was trying to get it, he knocked over a cup. The cup fell down and broke.

By comparing the answers given by the children, Piaget was able to investigate the reasons used by the children to assign blame, responsibility and punishment to each action. Younger children would typically say that John's action was worse because he broke many cups; whereas older children would say that Henry's action is worse because he should not take the jam without permission, or that John's action was not wrong because he did not know the chair was there.

Piaget found that younger children (around age four to seven) thought in terms of moral realism or **moral heteronomy**. These terms related to the fact that morality is seen in terms of rules that are fixed and unchangeable (heteronomy means 'from outside the person'). For example, guilt is determined by the extent of violation of rules rather than by the actual intention. Piaget found that even though five- to ten-year-old children were able to distinguish between deliberate and unintentional acts, they still tended to base their judgements on the outcome of the act: the worse the outcome, the worse the act. In this view a behaviour that has negative consequences will be judged as bad and as deserving of punishment, even if the intentions behind the action were good (Slavin, 2006). Because children think everybody has the same views about rules, the assumption is that rules are fixed external features of reality, rather than something that can be negotiated.

Around ten years of age children reach a second stage of moral development, called **autonomous morality**. It is at this point that children realise that rules are not fixed and arbitrarily imposed by others, but that they are created by consent. Children at this stage understand that they can change the rules of a game if others agree to do it. It is also at this stage that children are able to make judgements based on the person's motives: Henry was doing something he shouldn't have been doing, so his action is judged worse than John's action.

Although he differentiated several stages, Piaget did not see moral development as consisting of separate periods; instead, he sees development as progressing through two broad phases that overlap – so sometimes a child's moral reasoning will be in the heteronomous phase and at

Age	Stage	Key behaviours
Up to 4 years of age	Premoral judgement	▪ Rules are not understood ▪ No concept of morality
4–10 years	Moral heteronomy	▪ Rules come from higher authority and are unchangeable ▪ Evaluate actions by outcomes ▪ Punishments as inevitable retribution
10+	Moral autonomy	▪ Rules created by lots of people ▪ Evaluate actions by intentions ▪ Punishment as chosen to fit the crime

Table 8.1 Summary of Piaget's moral judgement phrases

other times it will be autonomous phase. Piaget also noted that the stages of moral understanding are not entirely discrete. Children become capable of certain autonomous judgements before others, depending on the people around them and the situation (Table 8.1).

The heteronomous phase

Key features of the child's heteronomous phase of moral understanding are beliefs that:

- Rules are handed down by authorities, such as God, parents and teachers.
- Rules are permanent and unchangeable and require strict obedience.
- Punishment should be proportional to the naughtiness of the behaviour. This is called '**expiatory punishment**'.
- Naughty behaviour will always be punished. This is called '**immanent justice**' – if you do something bad and later slip and hurt yourself then that is your punishment.

Moral understanding in the heteronomous phase is limited by:

- Adults who have the power to insist that children comply with rules without question
- The children's level of cognitive development, particularly egocentrism

The autonomous phase

During the autonomous phase of children's moral development their understanding moves towards an emphasis on intentions as more important than the consequences of action. Intentions form the basis for judging behaviour. At this stage children believe:

- That people differ in their moral reasoning
- Sometimes rules can be broken without negative consequences
- The punishment should fit the action, called 'reciprocal punishment'. There is no longer a belief in immanent justice.

Exposure to the views of others and a lack of egocentrism means that older children and adults are able to question their own moral views.

Gender in Piaget's theory of moral development

The main part of Piaget's investigation was with boys, either playing the game of marbles or based on reading stories and hearing their responses. Although he also observed the way girls played, his focus and main results and conclusions were based exclusively on boys. When comparing the games girls and boys played, Piaget found that the rules of the girls' games were not as complex as the boys and their marbles. Despite finding stages of moral heteronomy and autonomy in girls, Piaget stated that their games were less consistent in their organisation of rules, and they were more likely to relax them. Even though he acknowledged that these claims were based on superficial observations, the implication that girls' games appear less advanced and had less sophisticated moral understanding than boys has been heavily criticised. For example, Carol Gilligan (1982) criticised Piaget and other psychologists as harbouring negative views of feminine morality.

Evaluation

Piaget was a pioneer of moral development and the first to suggest a relationship between morality and cognitive development. However, Piaget's theories are not accepted without criticism as many researchers now dispute the ages and stages of his theory. For example, Colby and colleagues (1983) disagree with Piaget in that children's moral reasoning does not mature after the age of ten; similarly, children as young as three have been shown to alter the rules of games (Weston & Turiel, 1980).

Summary of Piaget's theory of moral development

- Children up to four years cannot understand rules.
- From four to ten, rules are seen as coming from higher authority and cannot be changed.
- At around ten years, rules are seen as mutually agreed by players.

Researchers have also criticised Piaget for underestimating very young children's ability in judging intentions and their understanding of punishment (Irwin & Moore, 1971). Another limitation is that by simply asking children their views, Piaget did not investigate how children actually behaved in practice. Instead, he assumed that the behaviour of a child would simply match their beliefs. In addition, there are criticisms of the dilemma stories used, for example they were uneven in consequences, listening to one and then another made demands on memory which may have affected outcomes and children have been found not to have a conception of rules as constraints.

Kohlberg's theory of morality

Lawrence Kohlberg (1927–1987) was a student of Piaget and, in principle, agreed with his theory of moral development, but wanted to develop his ideas further. Kohlberg saw moral development as a more gradual process than Piaget. Kohlberg developed his theory by analysing the responses children gave him after reading some stories, usually referred to as moral dilemmas: situations in which right and wrong actions are not always clear. Kohlberg was not concerned with whether the children decided that certain actions were right or wrong, but with their reasoning and how they arrived at their conclusions. Kohlberg's (1958) core sample included 72 boys, from both middle- and lower-class families in Chicago. They were ages 10, 13 and 16. He later added to his sample younger children, children who had been classified delinquents and boys and girls from other American cities and from other countries. The moral dilemma of 'Heinz' is one of his best known examples (Kohlberg, 1963, p. 19):

> *In Europe, a woman was near death from a special kind of cancer. There was one drug that the doctors thought might save her. It was a form of radium that a druggist in the same town had recently discovered. The drug was expensive to make, but the druggist was charging ten times what*

the drug cost him to make. He paid $200 for the radium and charged $2,000 for a small dose of the drug. The sick woman's husband, Heinz, went to everyone he knew to borrow the money, but he could only get together about $1,000 which is half of what it cost. He told the druggist that his wife was dying and asked him to sell it cheaper or let him pay for it later. But the druggist said: 'No, I discovered the drug and I'm going to make money from it'. So Heinz got desperate and broke into the man's store to steal the drug for his wife. Should the husband have done that?

Kohlberg was not really interested in whether the children said yes or no, but in the reasoning behind the answer. Following the story, Kohlberg would ask several questions trying to understand the rationale behind the answer. For example, Should Heinz steal the drug? Why or why not?, Does he or she have a duty or obligation to steal it?, Should he steal the drug if he does not love his wife?, Should he steal for a stranger?, It is illegal, is it morally wrong?

Based on his results, Kohlberg suggested the existence of three levels or stages, each one divided in two for a total of six stages, not only two as Piaget initially suggested.

Level 1: preconventional/premoral

This stage is similar to Piaget's first stage. Kohlberg also found that children follow fixed rules based on the authority of those who impose the rules.

Stage 1: obedience and punishment orientation

Kohlberg calls Stage 1 thinking 'preconventional'. Children respond to dilemmas such as that of 'Heinz' by responding that stealing is bad or that it is against the law. In addition, children suggest that the action is wrong because the person will be punished. Children in this stage see morality as something external to them.

Stage 2: naively egoistic orientation

Children in this stage usually report that a correct or right action is the action that satisfies the needs of the person and others around him. Children at this stage consider that what is correct is what is good for Heinz. Children in these stages usually refer to punishment at an individual level. The rules of the community or the society are not part of the reference for punishment. However, there are some similarities in the perception of punishment. In Stage 1 punishment is associated with being naughty, whereas in Stage 2 punishment is something we just want to avoid.

Level 2: conventional/role conformity

At this stage the moral values are associated to conforming to the correct role and to fulfilling the expectations of others.

Stage 3: good-boy/good-girl orientation

The main focus of the efforts of children at this stage is to conform to the stereotypical images of what a 'good' boy or girl is. Children try to achieve the expectations of the family and the community. Importantly, children at this stage appreciate intention, and actions are evaluated based on it. When questioned about Heinz, children may suggest that he was right to steal the drug because 'He was a good man for wanting to save his wife', or that 'Heinz's intentions were good'.

As mentioned before, there are similarities between the stages proposed by Piaget and Kohlberg. In both theories there is a shift from obedience to an involvement of intentions and motives.

Stage 4: authority and social-order-maintaining orientation

In Stage 4 the focus of the moral values of the child shifts to include the demands of the society as a whole. Children at this stage now view morality as a way in which each person has a role to play in the maintenance of social order. Children at this stage take decisions from the perspective of the society as a whole, so a typical response to the Heinz dilemma would be that they understand that the motives of Heinz are good, but they cannot condone theft. At this stage social order and respect to authority are seen as important not because of punishment but because they are good for the society.

Level 3: postconventional/self-accepted moral principles

Post-conventional morality is based on shared standards, rights and duties over and above the requirements of the authority. At this stage, the standards used are internal and actions and decisions are based on a rational process of thought concerning what is right or wrong.

Stage 5: contractual/legalistic orientation

The concerns at Stage 4 are related to the function and maintenance of society. In Stage 5 the shift is towards what is morally correct and makes a good society. People at this stage refer to rules and norms that make sense in rational terms and make society good. People understand that order is not good if it goes against the welfare of people and that norms can be broken based on doing a good action. At Stage 5 a response may defend Heinz's actions, arguing that it is his duty to save his wife and that a human life is more important than monetary gains.

Stage 6: The morality of individual principles of conscience

Stage 6 is characterised by an inclusion of the person's conscience in the decision of whether something or right or wrong. The main source of morality is internal and based on personal ideals and pressure to follow them. An important part of this stage is the understanding that a person should disobey laws that are not justified. Civil disobedience is a good example in which people follow their own code of morality disregarding the current law. The main difference between stages 5 and 6 is that in Stage 5 the person follows the social contract, whereas in Stage 6 the person uses his or her personal morals, even when they go against the law (Table 8.2).

Levels	Stages	Behaviours
Level 1: Pre-conventional morality	Stage 1 Reward punishment	Rules fixed and absolute; follow rules to avoid punishment
	Stage 2 Exchange	View and judge actions based on how they serve their individual needs
Level 2: Conventional morality	Stage 3 Good boy/good girl	Focus is on living up to social expectations (conformity)
	Stage 4 Law and order	Focus is on maintaining law and order by following rules, doing one's duty and respecting authority
Level 3: Post-conventional morality	Stage 5 Social contract	Rules of law for maintaining society must be agreed
	Stage 6 Universal principles	People follow internalised principles of justice

Table 8.2 Kohlberg's theory of moral development

Kohlberg followed up his original study every few years and in different countries, and found no differences to the results of his original proposal. However, he found that children in non-industrialised societies seemed to move more slowly through the stages of moral development. Importantly, a meta-analysis (a statistical combination of many studies) of studies performed in 27 different cultures found strong support for Kolberg's first four stages and in the progression suggested by Kohlberg. Unlike Piaget's theory, Kohlberg's ideas were revised and updated. He created a scoring system (the Standard Issue Scoring) and he dropped Stage 6 from his scoring manual, referring to it as a theoretical stage, and scoring all post-conventional responses as Stage 5 (Colby et al., 1983).

Evaluation

Similar to Piaget, Kohlberg only considered what the child believed and not the actions or behaviours of the children studied. Although the use of scenarios is positive, some people criticised his stories for being outside a child's experience in daily life and difficult to understand. The dilemmas used by Kohlberg were considered intuitive and unrealistic. Kurtines and Greif (1974) criticised the scoring scale as being unreliable and the 'clinical method' of interview as being very subjective.

Another limitation is the lack of support for stages 5 and 6. Results of comparative studies support the first four stages, but there is very little support for Stage 5 and almost none for Stage 6. Some people have suggested that there is no progression after Stage 4 (making this theory almost identical to Piaget's), and others suggested that stages 5 and 6 are the same. Kohlberg himself has concluded that his dilemmas are not useful for distinguishing between Stage 5 and Stage 6.

The strongest criticisms refer to the fact that the theory only focuses on cognitive development, concentrating purely on our thinking and reasoning, leaving emotions outside moral reasoning. In addition, the theory was criticised for being the result of research carried out primarily on boys. Finally, the analysis of Stage 5 strongly emphasised and place positive values on moral reasoning typical in individualistic Western societies unlike other societies in Asia and Africa. These latter societies are more focussed on collective values, putting the needs of the group in front of the needs of the individual.

> ## Summary of Kohlberg's theory of moral development
>
> - Pre-conventional morality (stages 1 and 2): The child follows rules to avoid punishments.
> - Conventional morality (stages 3 and 4): The child approaches problems in terms of his or her own position as good, responsible members of society.
> - Post-conventional morality (stages 5 and 6): The individual makes reasoned moral choices based on internalised universal moral principles.

Other theoretical models

Elliot Turiel has proposed a different theory of moral development, called the **moral domain theory**. In this theory, Turiel (1983) distinguishes between morality and other social conventions. For Turiel – in opposition to Kohlberg – morality is not the same as correctness. There are many social conventions that are viewed as socially correct or appropriate but they are not the same as morality. For Turiel, moral actions are based on the consequences that they bring to the person and others, focusing on ideas like harm, fairness and well-being. An important point of this theory is that it recognises that some actions are wrong (not moral) because they harm others, regardless of whether there is a rule that applied to the action. According to this theory, punching someone is wrong because the other person will be harmed, even if there was a rule 'accepting' hitting others (as in some boys' games).

Nancy Eisenberg and her colleagues proposed the theory of pro-social reasoning (Eisenberg, 2000). They presented dilemmas to children in which they have to take on the role of someone else and act either out of self-interest or in the interests of others. For example:

A girl named Mary was going to a friend's birthday party. On her way, she saw a girl who had fallen down and hurt her leg. The girl asked Mary to go to her home and get her parents so they could take her to the doctor. But if Mary did run and get the girl's parents, she would be late for the birthday party and miss the ice cream, cake and all the games.

Eisenberg was interested in how children reason when they have to face a conflict between their own needs and those of others. Crucial to her theory was the idea that morality develops alongside the emotional and cognitive developments of being able to empathise with others and being able to understand things from their point of view (see Chapter 6 and Chapter 7).

Eisenberg identified five main levels of pro-social reasoning:

1 *Hedonistic (self-focused) orientation.* The child only cares for him or herself. Any altruistic behaviour is motivated by selfishness or expectations of reciprocity (I will help now, so they help me later), or simply because the child likes the person they are helping (Mary should help because the girl is nice).

2 *Needs of others orientation.* The needs of the specific situation are being addressed rather than a genuine sense of empathy. When asked, the child offers simple explanations for their positive behaviour without referring to the need of role-taking (Mary should help because the girl is hurt).

3 *Stereotyped orientation or approval-focused orientation.* The child's actions are based on gaining the approval of others, so the child acts in a way that will make him or her liked. When asked to explain their behaviour they tend to use stereotyped portrayals of good and bad behaviour (Helping others is good).

4 *Empathic orientation.* The child shows perspective-taking and genuine empathy by putting him or herself in the shoes of others. There are feelings of genuine guilt when considering his or her own actions. The actions now include wider social values when the child puts him or herself in the place of others. Concepts like 'dignity' and 'rights' are present in the perspective-taking process.

5 *Internalised orientation.* The responsibilities towards others based on moral obligations, norms and values are used when a child has to act. Some wider social conditions may be present (requirements related to equality, obligation and honour).

The child who has reached the internalised orientation stage has a full set of social values and understands their responsibilities towards others. Importantly, not all children reach or progress to these stages at the same time. In summary, the child moves from a level of self-focused concerns (egocentric), to one which conforms to social norms. Finally, these norms are internalised into the reasoning of the child.

There are some limitations of this theory. For example, in more collectivist cultures some children show Stage 5 reasoning, even when they are very young and could not have progressed through the other stages. In addition, there is no mention of rewards and punishments present in other theories and this theory has no clear predictions about these reinforcers.

A proponent of behaviourism, Skinner (1972) focused on socialisation as the primary force behind moral development. Skinner focused on the power of external forces (reinforcement contingencies) to shape an individual's development. Social learning theory suggests that moral behaviour is learned like any other behaviour based on observational learning and reinforcement and punishment. The more rewarded we are when we perform a behaviour the more we will do it. Parents and caregivers consistently reinforce positive behaviours to children.

Conclusion

There are many similarities and differences in the moral theories presented and research has yet to show conclusively whether one is better than others. Each theory has benefits and limitations. Given the complexity of the topic and the several processes and stages involved, it is likely that these theories complement each other.

Chapter 9

Social Learning

The social development of a child begins as soon as the child enters into the world. Developing language to communicate and understanding one's own and others' emotions is particularly important in being able to develop social relationships and to successfully interact. In fact, the relationships children establish with their parents and siblings during the first two years are crucial, and these early bonds set the blueprint to the child's future relationships. As a child enters schools, peers become more influential.

In this chapter, we will examine:
- Early social behaviours
- The importance of family and siblings to a child's social development
- Attachment and the internal working model
- Characteristics of friendships
- Gender differences in social relationships
- The nature of aggression between children and its relationship to friendship and popularity

👁 Early social behaviour and social interactions

The human infant appears fairly helpless at birth, relying on others to provide for all its basic needs. However, the infant does have some abilities to help the development of social interactions. Amongst these abilities are behaviours for social situations. Auditory and visual stimulation has been shown to be especially attractive to infants and they are designed to interact with adults and to give the infant an initial orientation to social situations (Smith, Cowie & Blades, 2008). Newborn babies will both smile and cry but this behaviour has no social meaning. Gradually the child will learn the social consequences of smiling and crying because of the responses caregivers give to them. For example, a game such as peek-a-boo is initially played mostly by the adult trying to surprise the child with the sudden appearance/disappearance of a face. The child's enjoyment becomes more genuine as he or she takes a more active part. Babies also already have the ability to learn and from the first months of life, infants are discriminating social stimuli and learning the consequences of social actions. Imitation of social stimuli occurs between 6–12 months of age (Barr, Dowden & Haye, 1996).

Summary

- Newborn babies have some abilities for the development of social interactions, namely:
- Behaviours which operate primarily in social situations
- Behaviours to which social responses are given
- An enjoyment in being responded to
- An ability to learn

👁 Early social relationships and theory of mind

During the first few months the child and the caregiver normally engage in long and repeated periods of face-to-face interaction. These interactions help to expand the child's attention to the environment and objects following the direction of another person to the object of interest. Face-to-face interactions may help the infant to detect similarities and dissimilarities between motor behaviours and emotional expressions, and between the self and other people during the interaction (Gergely & Watson, 1999).

Findings continually relate richer social interactions as a precursor to development of theory of mind (ToM), suggesting that social interactions in which the child engages are critical to ToM development. For example, three- to four-year-old children with a sibling pass a standard false belief task, an index of ToM, earlier than children without siblings (Jenkins & Astington, 1996). Children who have older siblings close to them in age and who interact frequently with each other are more likely to pass false belief tasks (Taumoepeau & Reese, 2013). Both increased opportunities for joint attention and social referencing are thought to contribute to earlier ToM abilities.

Children's performances are also influenced by the relationship between the mother and older sibling. Youngblade and Dunn (1995) noted that mothers and siblings talk about feelings with children differently. Mothers focus on discussing children's feelings, whilst siblings focus on shared feelings when playing or teasing. The fact that children with older siblings receive social information, not only from multiple sources but in a fashion that is complementary rather than redundant, helps the younger sibling to pass false belief tasks at an earlier age than those children without an older sibling. Taken together, increased pretend play, other-focused conflict resolution and discussion of emotions in positive relationships during the first three years of life significantly increases performance on false belief in children with older siblings.

◉ Attachment

Attachment theory is focused on long-term relationships between people. An attachment means a bond or tie between a child and an attachment figure, more likely the mother. These bonds are based on the child's need for safety, security and protection, all of them very important in childhood. Children become attached to responsive adults who interact with them and remain as consistent caregivers, usually from six months to two years. Children use attachment figures as a base to explore their surroundings. When the child starts to crawl, he or she will explore the environment using the attachment figure as a 'secure base' where the child can safely return to. The responses of the caregiver will help the development of attachment as well as the confidence to explore new situations and places. When the figure is not present, a sense of grief is experience by the child, called separation anxiety. This response is considered to be a normal and adaptive response for an attached infant (Benoit, 2004).

Summary

- Attachment is an affectional bond in which the presence of the figure adds a special sense of security, a 'safe base' for the child individual

- Attachments behaviours create and maintain proximity and strengthen the bond with the caregiver

◎ Early ideas of attachment

Attachment theory in psychology originates with the work of John Bowlby (1958). John Bowlby developed his theory when working as a psychiatrist for emotionally disturbed children. Bowlby observed that children experienced intense distress when separated from their mothers. The importance of the bond between the mother and child was further highlighted by the fact the child remained anxious even when being fed. This went against the view held at the time that an attachment is formed when basic needs such as food and warmth are provided. Other researchers using rhesus monkeys found that physical contact was a necessity (Harlow & Zimmerman, 1958). Harry Harlow did a number of studies on attachment in monkeys, suggesting that monkeys must form their attachments during the first year of life – called a critical period). He reared monkeys in two different conditions: in isolation or with surrogate mothers. Monkeys reared in isolation were frightened, behaved abnormally and could not interact with other monkeys even when they were older. The monkeys with surrogate mothers had access to two types: a bare wire dummy mother with a feeding bottle attached to it and a wire dummy covered in soft terry towelling cloth. The monkeys spent more time with the cloth mother and they would only go to the wire mother when they were hungry. Once fed, the monkeys would return to the cloth mother for most of the day. If a frightening object was placed in the cage, the monkey took refuge with the cloth mother. These findings support the evolutionary theory of attachment, it is the sensitive response and security of the caregiver that is important. Harlow's work has been criticised as his experiments have been seen as unnecessarily cruel, unethical and of limited value in attempting to understand the effects of deprivation on human infants (Gluck, Bell & Pearson-Bish, 2003).

Bowlby was strongly influenced by Harlow's research. According to Bowlby, infants have a universal need to seek close proximity with their caregiver when under stress or threatened (Prior & Glaser, 2006). Attachment is adaptive as it enhances the infant's chance of survival. Bowlby suggested that a child would initially form only one primary attachment (monotropy) which would provide a safe base for the child to explore the world. Their relationship with the attachment figure was thought to provide a mould which a child would use to base other future social relationships. This theory also suggests that there is a critical period for developing attachment and that if attachment to a figure has not developed during this period then the child will suffer from irreversible developmental consequences.

Bowlby described four stages in the development of attachment which has subsequently been extended to a fifth.

1 *Birth to about three months:* infants orient to social stimuli (i.e. voices and faces) but are not yet able to discriminate amongst individuals.
2 *At about five to seven months:* infants orient and respond to one person (typically the mother).
3 *From about seven to nine months:* mobility allows infants to actively maintain proximity to the attachment figure.
4 *From two or three years of age on:* children begin to have awareness of the mother's feelings so the attachment develops into a partnership (goal-corrected partnership).
5 *At school age or older:* lessening of attachment. The direct bond is replaced with more abstract relationships such as affection, trust and approval.

Much of more recent refinement of attachment theory was informed by Mary Ainsworth's innovative methodology and observational studies. Using Bowlby's early formulation, she conducted observational research on infant–parent pairs during the child's first year, combining extensive home visits with the study of behaviours in particular situations. She devised a laboratory-based procedure known as the Strange Situation protocol to measure children's behaviour to being separated and reunited with a caregiver. By creating stresses designed to activate attachment behaviour, the procedure assesses how children use their caregiver as a safe base.

In the Strange Situation, the carer and child are placed in an unfamiliar playroom while a researcher records specific behaviours, observing through a one-way mirror. In eight different episodes, the child experiences separations and reunions from the carer and the presence of a stranger. Ainsworth identified three attachment styles that a child may have with attachment figures: secure, anxious-avoidant (insecure) and anxious-ambivalent or resistant (insecure). The type of attachment developed by infants depends on the quality of care they have previously received (Ainsworth, Blehar, Waters & Wall, 1978). Each of the attachment patterns is associated with certain characteristic patterns of behaviour. The three outlined by Ainsworth following the Strange Situation procedure were as follows:

- *Secure*: Parents were assessed as being generally responsive and sensitive towards their children. The child misses the parent on the separation stage, but greets the parent on their return with a smile, conversation or gesture and then returned to the activity that they were engaged in while the parent was absent, or if upset seeks comfort from their parent.
- *Insecure avoidant*: Parents were assessed as being rejecting and/or interfering. The child shows little distress on the separation stage and actively avoids or ignores the parent on their return. If picked up, the child stiffens and leans away. Therefore the child is seen as seeking distance from the parent.
- *Insecure ambivalent*: Parents were assessed as behaving inconsistently towards the child. When the parents return the child finds no comfort from the presence of the parent, either greeting the parent with angry rejection, tantrums, or appearing extremely upset.

Further research by Mary Main and Judith Solomon (1986) identified a fourth attachment pattern, called *disorganised/disoriented attachment*. The name reflects these children's lack of a coherent coping strategy, displaying disoriented behaviours such as approaching the returning adult but with the back turned. Very often this style is associated with children who have suffered some sort of abuse (Main, 1990).

In Mary Ainsworth's original study 65% of children tested exhibited a secure pattern, 21% the avoidant pattern and 14% the ambivalent pattern. These proportions have been replicated in 39 studies in eight different countries. However, in a small number of countries such as Japan, a relatively high number of infants in the Strange Situation show insecure ambivalent behaviours (Sagi, Van IJzendoorn & Koren-Karie, 1991). This has led to criticisms that the Strange Situation protocol may be more stressful for Japanese babies and secure attachments in that culture may be characterised differently.

Research has since sought to ascertain the extent to which a parent's attachment classification is predictive of their children's classification.

Parents' perceptions of their own childhood attachments were found to predict their children's classifications 75% of the time (Fonagy, Steele & Steele, 1991).

Bowlby's original theory was criticised for focusing too much on the mother as the caregiver. Criticisms of Ainsworth's Strange Situation analysis focus on the development of a classification based on inadequate sample sizes and that what was considered 'normal' behaviour to signal the secure attachment type differs culturally. In addition, the procedure only measures the relationship between the mother and the child, and less research has been conducted between child and other caregivers (Waters, Petters & Facompre, 2013).

Summary

- Attachments form an important part of child's emotional development.
- Mary Ainsworth identified three types of attachment according to the Strange Situation: secure, insecure ambivalent and insecure avoidant.
- Later, researcher Main and Solomon (1986) added a fourth attachment style called disorganised-insecure attachment based upon their own research.

◉ Parental emotional availability and attachment

A crucial component for secure attachment is emotional availability. When parents are emotionally 'reachable' and are able to 'read' the emotional signals of their children, the children will perform better in a wide variety of situations. Someone is considered emotionally available if they can't be distracted by their own emotions. Research has consistently shown that more emotional availability in mother–infant interactions predicted more secure infant–mother attachments (Cassibba, van Ijzendoorn & Coppola, 2012).

Mothers of secure infants have been rated as being more sensitive, responsive, accessible and co-operative during the first year of the child's development than those of insecure infants. An increasing number of studies have also shown secure infants to be more competent in both their cognitive and social skills (Sroufe, 2005). When parents are unresponsive or not emotionally available children are at risk for developing insecure attachments. Children who are medically ill and also those of depressed mothers have been found to be more vulnerable to insecure attachment, showing mixed pattern of avoidant and ambivalent/resistant. Maltreated or abused children typically show disorganised attachment. This has led to the suggestion that disorganisation is a very insecure pattern of attachment and may have implications for subsequent psychopathology (Pasalich, Dadds, Hawes & Brennan, 2012).

Summary

- The two main factors affect the attachment relationship are emotional availability and caregiver sensitivity.
- Maltreated and children of depressed mothers are at risk of developing insecure attachment.

⟨◉⟩ Attachment and the internal working model

Attachment styles rarely change across the lifespan and infant attachment status has an effect on later social development. This is called the 'internal working model' (IWM) and refers to the cognitive construction of relationships, such as expectations of support or affection, trust etc. According to Bowlby, those with secure IWMs expect people to be supportive and they behave in an open way which elicits such support. Those with insecure IWMs are less trusting and do not expect good care and nor believe they are worthy of good care. Their distrust, coldness or hostility can elicit more negative responses from others, which in turn confirms their belief that they are not worthy of care. The way adults think about their attachment experiences correlates with how they parent their own children, how they relate to other people, some clinical outcomes, some criminal/antisocial outcomes and also their behaviour in romantic relationships. Following up infants who were rated secure or insecure at age one year, Bretherton (1985) observed them at age two in a nursery setting. Secure infants had greater attention span, more positive emotion and used tools confidently. Insecure-ambivalent children were less socially able, more dependent upon the teacher; whereas insecure-avoidant infants were found to be more hostile and distant with peers. A child's attachment style will often predict the parent's own attachment style.

There is also a strong relationship between the mother's attachment and the attachment style of the child due to the mother's behaviour towards the child, which varies as a result of her own working model (Steele, Hodges, Kaniuk, Hillman & Henderson, 2003).

Insecure attachment has also been found to lead to problems with intimate adult relationships and the pursuit of intimacy through inappropriate sexual behaviour in adulthood. Although insecure attachment is hypothesised to be a vulnerability factor for criminality in general, Marshall (1989) was one of the first to suggest that insecure attachment in childhood would lead to difficulties establishing intimate adult relationships. Craissati, McClurg and Browne (2002) found a high prevalence of a history of affectionless, controlling style of parenting as reported by adult sexual offenders of their own parents (using a standardised test and structured interview). They also report some evidence suggesting that low parental care was associated with childhood abuse. Physical and sexual abuse are also highly likely to occur when there is home life characterised by poor parental relationships, a history of parental aggression, alcohol abuse and criminality. Finally, Smallbone and McCabe (2003) found that sexual offenders who reported an insecure attachment style to their own parents were also found more likely to report being sexually abused compared to those with a secure attachment style.

Summary

- The internal working model is a set of cognitive representations of the caregiver's responsiveness and accessibility. According to Bowlby, the IWM influences how the baby behaves in the Strange Situation and how the child relates to people in later development.
- The IWM is built up by the first intimate relationship in life (with the caregiver) and provides the initial template for all future close relationships.
- The IWM of relationships influences interactions in childhood, romantic interactions, responses to parents and how you parent your own children.

◉ Friends and school

In the early stages of social development, the family teaches children how to interact with others and what is or is not acceptable. However, as children enter primary school the focus of the child's social world moves away from the family, and the child's peer groups becomes the most important feature (Ladd, 1990). A peer group is often characterised by sharing similarities with each other such as age, background and social status. Peers have been shown to be especially interesting to other children and this has been observed in infants as early as 12–18 months. Interactions with peers help to increase the skills of infants attending day nurseries and by children having a secure attachment style (Nix, Bierman, Domitrovich & Gill, 2013). Imitation has also been found to aid peer skills.

Play

Children learn a lot about themselves through play and they also learn important social skills. From two years of age there is a dramatic increase in children's social skills and play, usually through four stages:

1 *Solitary play* – describes the play style when a child is around other children but is playing alone not paying attention to others. At this stage, infants and young toddlers learn through their senses and explore toys, objects and people by looking, touching, grasping and tasting. They enjoy mainly interactions with caregivers in basic interactions such as peek-a-boo.

2 *Parallel play* – occurs as young children become more aware of other children, around two years of age. They explore their environment and enjoy playing with toys independently. Whilst they see themselves as part of social group, they tend to play next to each other with the same game or activities rather than playing together.

3 As children develop more interest in their peers and more skills to interact with others, they enter the *associative play* stage. At this stage, children may play the same game with one another, but are not necessarily working together. They enjoy watching their peers and imitating others, but have limited interaction while playing together.

4 *Group play* – By the age of three, children are more able to communicate and socialise with others. Their language has developed so that those outside the family are able to share ideas with them. Through interactive play they begin to learn social skills such as sharing and taking turns. They also develop the ability to collaborate on the 'theme' of the play activity (Figure 9.1).

Figure 9.1 Solitary play, parallel play and group play

From three years on the main emphasis continues to be on group play. The size of the group they play with increases into middle school. There are also differences with who the child plays with as they increase in age. At around six years old there is an increase in sex segregation, the tendency of children to associate with others of the same sex.

Gender segregation begins as early as two to three years of age with children being more interactive and sociable when playing with same-sex friends. In addition, when with the opposite sex, they tend to watch or play alongside the other child rather than interact directly. Gender segregation is very prominent after the age of three, and preschool children spend very little time playing one-on-one with the opposite sex. They spend some time in mixed-sex groups but spend most of their time playing with same-sex peers. Some researchers believe that gender segregation occurs because children seek partners whose play styles match or complement their own. For example, in toddlers and young children, the first to segregate tend to be the most active and disruptive boys and the most socially sensitive girls (Serbin, Moller, Gulko, Powlishta & Colburne, 1994). At around three, children also develop concepts or ideas (schemas) about what boys and girls are typically like. These concepts include stereotyped, and often exaggerated, notions about gender differences: 'Boys are rough and like to fight and play with trucks' and 'Girls are nice and like to talk and play with dolls'.

Summary

- Play develops in four stages.
- Gender segregation appears at around three years and markedly increases at around six years of age.

Peer structure

Understanding peer group structure and its relevance for young people's behaviour has been enhanced by the use of sociometric techniques. A sociometric questionnaire is an instrument that asks respondents to name or identify group members who satisfy a preference criterion such as liking or similarity. Sociometry allows investigators to build up a map of relationships within a social system, such as a school year group, based on friendship nominations; and to identify pupils in different sociometric positions such as groups, dyads, 'hangers-on' and isolates. For example, high levels of aggression and withdrawal and low levels of sociability and cognitive abilities result in 'rejected' individuals. Coie and Dodge (1983) found that 30% of those 'rejected' remained so and another 30% became 'highlighted'. Good interpersonal skills and low levels of aggression result in 'popular' children. Popularity and aggression is a complicated combination as 'controversial' children are quite aggressive but not disliked by the rest of the group, although they can display higher levels of aggression in adolescence.

Importance of friendship

Having close friends is extremely important to a child's development. Field (1984) showed children as young as four to show a 'grief response' when children left kindergarten to go to primary schools. Also, having friends has been found to increase altruism and self-esteem. In general friendship is associated with reciprocity, intimacy, more social activities, less conflict and more pretend play and problem-solving among children.

Adolescence is a period during which great social differentiation takes place. Although adolescents are still close to their parents, they spend more time with their friends and their physical and emotional dependence is transferred from the parents to their peers. Harris (1998) found that the peer group is the most important environmental factor influencing the personality and development of adolescents. A number of studies confirm the importance of the peer group with regard to personality development. Budhall (1998) identified a strong relationship between social isolation among peers and low self-esteem in adolescents, while Bagwell, Newcomb, and Bukowski (1998) concluded that rejection by the peer group was a significant predictor of social adjustment after a period of 12 years.

Chapter 10

Developmental Psychopathology

In its simplest terms, psychopathology can be considered behaviour that is atypical to that accounted by others of a similar age and culture, is of long-lasting duration not sufficiently explained by a recent trauma or stress (loss of a family member, family divorce) and impacts on everyday life (Cicchetti, 2014).

The time frame in which psychopathology develops is usually considered in relation to various contexts (biological, individual, family, social and cultural). The biological context explains deviant development based on genetics, biochemistry, brain structure and neurological functioning as well as innate individual differences (temperament). The individual context concerns psychological variables within the person such as personality characteristics, thought processes and emotions. The family context is also important, particularly in the case of child development, with the greatest attention being paid the parent–child relationship. Widening relationships further we also need to consider social relations

In this chapter, we will examine:
- Models of child psychopathology that have been proposed to account for the cause of psychopathology
- Continuum between atypical and normal development
- Risk, resilience and protective factors
- Methods of diagnosing psychopathology
- Development of common childhood psychopathologies (ASD, anxiety and depression)

outside the family such as peers, teachers and adult role models. Cultural context is also important to how the child develops, as factors such as socioeconomic status, race and ethnicity all impact on the risk of psychopathology. It is the interaction of all these factors that heightens a person's chance of developing psychopathology (Uher, 2014).

Models of child psychopathology

A variety of models of the **etiology** (origins of cause) of childhood psychopathology have been put forward. Each of these models maps on to concepts which have already been introduced in the key theories of development in previous chapters. Each model contains distinctive features but also shares common features with the others (Kerig, Ludlow & Werner, 2012). Whilst each model has considerable strengths, none have been found to be totally satisfactory in accounting for developmental psychopathology. The main models put forward are:

- The medical model
- The behavioural model
- Social learning theory
- Cognitive models
- Psychoanalytic models
- The family systemic model

We will now look at the key features of these models in depth.

The medical model

The medical model works on the basis that psychopathologies are a result of organic dysfunction – whether as a function of neurochemistry, brain structure or neuropsychological functioning. The medical model therefore retains a view that psychopathology is an illness residing within a person, rather than a product of dynamic interactions between the child and the environment. The medical model is largely built around biological factors as a cause, with psychological processes such as stress or exposure to trauma also affecting biology. The medical model classifies behaviour problems in medical terms as 'physical illnesses'.

Neurotransmitters are the brain chemicals which act like a telephone wire and communicate signals around the body and brain. When the transmitters are unbalanced there will be problems with over excitement or inhibition of actions. Serotonin seems to be the most important and widely researched neurotransmitter, too much serotonin is thought to contribute to atypical development or be stuck in a constant euphoric state where they are too happy, too little will cause depression and suicidal thoughts. Dopamine is the 'reward' chemical, too much can cause fetishes, sexual addiction, over eating, too little can also cause anxiety and depression. Drugs that increase and/or decrease the transmitters to a more normal balance are often used as treatments of the disorder. For example, children with depression may have low levels of dopamine and certain medications will be able to increase the levels of dopamine.

The brain is made up of three main structures: the cerebrum (the forebrain), the cerebellum (the hindbrain) and the brain stem. The cerebellum is the largest area of the brain and controls all higher mental functions, such as thinking and memory. It is made up of two hemispheres, left and right. The left hemisphere controls the right side of the body and vice versa. The hemispheres are further divided into four lobes (occipital, parietal, temporal and frontal). Each has it is own function: the occipital is largely responsible for visual information (colour and shape); the parietal for spatial information and language; the temporal lobes for auditory and emotional information; the frontal lobes are involved in planning, memory and thought. Different psychopathologies have been linked with different structural damage. For example, autism has been linked to an atypical balance between the right and left sides of the corpus callosum. Even though children with autism are more likely to be left-handed they do not show the left side of the corpus callosum to be dominant (Brandler & Paracchini, 2014). In children with attention hyperactivity disorder, who have problems in planning and monitoring of their behaviour, abnormal activity in the frontal lobes has been reported (Noreika, Falter & Rubia, 2013).

The behavioural model

The behaviourists believe that once allowance has been made for genetic, maturational and temperamental factors all behaviour should conform to the basic principles of learning: classical conditioning, operant conditioning and imitation (Chapter 3). Behaviourists assume that all behaviours are observable and through this process of observation we should be able to predict and modify these behaviours.

For example, some children grow up with the kinds of learning experiences that increase their chances of adapting well to different environmental demands. Here, positive behaviours have been rewarded and modelled, and negative ones have been suppressed. In a child at risk of psychopathology the opposite patterns are likely to have occurred. Maladaptive behaviours are the ones that are rewarded and modelled and positive ones have been extinguished either through lack of reinforcement or through punishment. The context of these behaviours is important to note, as what is adaptive to one society may be seen a maladaptive to another.

In order to consider these different cultural standards, deviations in behaviour can be defined in terms of frequency or intensity of behaviour compared to what is usually expected depending on the culture. In behaviour deficit, behaviours occur at a lower frequency or intensity to what is expected, so the child's social, intellectual or practical skills are impaired. Examples of psychopathology in which a behaviour deficit are observed include children with autism and learning difficulties. Behaviour **excess** is when a behaviour occurs at a higher frequency or intensity than is adaptive to the standards of the child's culture. Examples include the hyperactive child who is in constant state of anxiety or the obsessive compulsive child who repeatedly washes their hands. Finally, the developmental dimension considers age-related changes that also need to be noted. For example, the age in which children stop feeding from their mother or learn to walk differs depending on the culture.

Social learning theory

Bandura (1986) and other social theorists expanded on the behavioural theorists. He believed the person and environment to influence each other. He also highlighted the importance of attention and cognitive processes, such as internal representations of experiences, expectancies and problem solving. These internal representations determine which events will be observed, their interpretation and how they will be used in the future. Bandura (1977) also introduced the concept of self-efficacy, the fact that individuals come to anticipate not only a given behaviour will produce a given outcome, but whether or not they can successfully execute such a behaviour. People fear and avoid situations that they believe exceed their coping skills, and they behave with confidence in those situations which they believe themselves capable of coping with.

Self-efficacy influences both the choice of action and persistence in the face of obstacles.

Cognitive models

In Chapters 3 and 5 you were introduced to the leading cognitive psychologists including Piaget. Piaget's cognitive theory in particular has been used to attempt to map the development of psychopathology. For example, he proposed that there is a fixed order of stages of development, and no higher order thinking occurs until a child progresses through that stage.

An important aspect of Piaget's work was the concept of a schema, the blueprint through which a child begins to understand their environment. The child uses this schema to build up their knowledge to gain more complex ways of thinking. Assimilation accounts for incorporation of new information into existing schema. For example, a child who is always left out of games with siblings may be cautious with other children if the schema they develop is 'all children will not like me'. Accommodation refers to changing this schema to take account of new information – a child may adjust his or her schema if, when starting school for example, children allow him or her to play with them; the schema may be adapted to 'not all children will dislike me'.

Whereas normative development is characterised by a balance or equilibration, of assimilation and accommodation, problems arise when accommodation and assimilation are used to the exclusion of one another. Exclusive use of assimilation will interfere with new learning, leading a child to make erroneous assumptions and to distort information so that it fits with pre-existing notions. A child overly reliant on accommodation may be lost in fantasy, bending the world to their wishes. Exclusive use of accommodation would result in a child constantly changing his or her schema to fit with new stimuli.

Social cognition

Social information processing models also can explain how cognition may influence psychopathology. When solving social problems children go through a series of steps: encoding, interpretation, searching responses, selecting response, acting on response (Crick & Dodge, 1994). They will then make an attribution, inference about cause of behaviour. In a disturbed child the cognitive process is thought to be either disturbed or deficient.

Aggressive children are predisposed to attribute malicious intent to others even when an action or behaviour is completely accidental or non-intentional. This is also referred to as the hostile attribution bias.

Psychoanalytic models

Classical psychoanalysis, also known as drive theory, is concerned with discovering the dynamics – the basic motives – that drive our behaviour. In Chapter 3, we covered one of the leading contributions to psychoanalytic theory: Sigmund Freud's structural model and his psychosexual theory. We now return to these theories in turn to discuss how they could account for psychopathology.

The structural model

The model put forward by Freud introduced the concepts of the id, ego and superego. The id ('it') is the source of all biological drives and basic needs, the ego ('me') represents the need to balance gratification with reality and the superego ('over-me') represents moral standards. According to the structural model, psychopathology is a matter of internal conflict and imbalance between id, ego and superego. If the id is excessively strong, the result is impulsive aggressive or sexual behaviour. If the superego is excessively strong, the result is overly inhibited behaviour in which the child feels guilty about anything they consider to have done wrong or differently to what they think is expected to them.

The psychosexual theory

Whilst much of the content of Freud's ideas surrounding psychosexuality is not considered relevant today, the developmental process he put forward is still important. In terms of psychopathology, fixations are key to developmental process by which psychopathology occurs. Fixations result in disturbances either because they hamper further development or because they increase the chances of the child returning to fixated, less mature stages when stressed (regression) (Kerig, Ludlow & Werner, 2012). The stage in which the fixation occurs will determine the severity and the kind of psychopathology; the earlier the fixation, the more severe the psychopathology.

Ego psychology

Erikson (1950) emphasised that the ego can operate independently of the id. Ego psychology is based largely around Erikson's psychosocial theory already covered in Chapter 3. Erikson's developmental model focuses on the stages of psychosocial development running parallel to Freud's developmental stages. Erickson proposed that each stage (trust versus mistrust, autonomy versus shame, initiative versus guilt, industry versus inferiority, identity versus confusion) represents a crisis, the resolution of which sets the individual on a particular developmental trajectory .Erikson laid out clear stages and tasks that a child need to successfully achieve to proceed normally to the next stage, as well as including a social context in which child development takes place.

The family systemic model

Whilst many other theories highlight the importance of the family, the family systemic model is special as it considers the family as a unit. The family is considered a 'system' to reflect the fact relationships within the family are coherent and stable. The core idea is that individual personality is a function of the family system.

Minuchin (1974; Minuchin, Lee & Simon, 2006) put forward the structural family theory. He believed being part of a family helped us to develop through participating in a number of relationships at the same time. Within the family system, there are naturally occurring subsystems that join family members as well as differentiate each other. For instance, parents form a marital subsystem, based on their combined roles as mother and father and romantic couple, they raise children and play a leadership role. The parent–child relationship is another subsystem – children turn to parents for comfort and advice, parents expect their authority to be respected. Sibling relationships are another subsystem which differ depending on the birth order of the child. For example, older children may have roles defined by special privileges or be subject to different expectations. Through these various roles, family members experience feelings of belonging and independence from each other.

What allows the subsystems to function well are the boundaries that separate them. Clear boundaries define the roles of individuals in order to meet developmental needs. They change through development so parent–child relationships become more reciprocal and equal as the child heads towards adulthood.

When appropriate boundaries are not maintained families becomes dysfunctional. Whilst rigid boundaries can provide a sense of self-sufficiency they make it difficult for family members to communicate and to display emotions with each other. At the other extreme, absent, unstable or unclear boundaries result in enmeshment, there is no differentiation between the family roles. The child may be forced to grow up too quickly. They are treated like an adult and forced to have to look after themselves or even their parents.

⦿ Distinguishing non-psychopathological developmental problems from psychopathology

When looking at behavioural, cognitive or emotional characteristics associated with psychopathology, many characteristics can be also observed in children considered to be developing normally. Consider the following examples:

A young infant refusing to sleep through the night and constantly screams and cries despite not wanting to eat or be changed.

A child who screams and kicks like a rabid animal every time they are not allowed what they want.

A child who will constantly seek reassurance from other people, and will always choose to play with a few select friends. They may be shy and awkward when meeting new people.

A child who grabs an object they want from others and may hit, kick or scream themselves blue in the face from time to time. Or a child who withdraws into themselves when introduced to new situations.

A child who fails to co-operate with others, shows a flippant attitude and complete disregard for rules. They may become volatile over minute things that never bothered them before.

A child who jumps in to new things without thinking, simply follows the crowd and tends not to think of the consequences of their actions. Everything becomes a drama when they don't get their way.

A child who over-differentiates their feelings and believes they are the only ones capable of experiencing their own unique emotions, constantly expressing the sentiment 'Nobody understands me'.

Every one of the examples above thought to represent a child going through a normal stage of development. However, which important feature of each of the children in these seven examples would make a psychologist more confident in their assessment that the behaviour is normal?

Ages and stages in development

You would probably not think twice if you were told the child who regularly cries if they don't get want they want and will throw themselves on the floor of the shop in protest, kicking and screaming, is two. You can assume that the child is simply exerting their independence as they go through the 'terrible twos'. However, if you were instead told that child was 13 years of age we are sure that you would have stopped and thought for longer. This is because any typically developing child would have outgrown this stage and would be aware that it would be inappropriate behaviour particularly when out in public. Take another example: a child who has started going out with friends and drinking and smoking. You would be less alarmed if you knew the child was 15 but if you were told they were only eight years old then concerns would no doubt be raised.

Throughout the book we have introduced an assortment of different theories to account for a child's behaviour in various domains whether cognitive, social or emotional. Whilst some theories are more concrete in what they classify as fixed stages in development in which certain behaviours occur, key to all theories is that there are certain behaviours associated with different stages of a child's development. While it is acknowledged throughout this book that children develop at varying rates and that there is normal variation in the ages children may achieve particular developmental milestones, this variation lies within particular ranges that are acknowledged to be the 'normal range'. When development occurs outside of those normal ranges on the extreme ends of a continuum then psychopathology is suspected.

One important characteristic of developmental psychopathology is that it assumes that there is a continuum between normal and abnormal development. Development psychopathology occurs because development has gone awry at one of these stages. The importance is then to identify why development takes one path rather than another healthier one.

👁 Risk and resilience

A risk factor is any circumstance or condition that increases the chances of psychopathology developing. There are vast numbers of risk factors and they appear in many different contexts. Biological risks factors can include genetic disorders, prenatal injury and nutrition. Individual risk factors include cognitive deficits, low self-esteem and poor behavioural control. Family risk factors include interparental conflict, abuse, neglect, domestic violence, parental psychopathology, insecure working models of attachment. Cultural factors include poverty, prejudice, community and violence.

Child development is incredibly complex and any potential risk factor is rarely a static agent. It is not usually the case that a simple cause–effect relationship (e.g., physical abuse causes depression) is able to account for psychopathology alone. Instead, it is important to also understand the mechanism in which these risk factors exert their negative effects. There are a number of risk mechanisms underlying psychopathology including insecure attachments and distorted schemas.

Whereas a risk factor would be expected to negatively affect any child exposed to it, vulnerability is thought to increase the likelihood that a particular child will succumb to risk. One example of a vulnerability factor is gender. Whilst stress has negative effect on children's behaviour for both boys and girls, boys react with an excessive amount of behaviour problems compared to girls. Temperament is another, as a child with a difficult temperament is not only more reactive to stress but is also more likely to be the cause of additional stress in family.

👁 Protective factors and mechanisms

The term developmental pathway is used to account for psychopathology across the lifespan (Pickles & Hill, 2006). Development pyschopathologists attempt to address at what point in time and for what reasons development begin to go awry and explain why not all at risk children become disturbed. Therefore it is as important to identify those at risk who do go on to develop the disorder as well as the children who continue to develop normally. Equally, as some children stay on a disordered course (continuity), others are deflected on to healthy pathway (discontinuity) – effectively growing out of it. Understanding the mechanisms that propel a child from one pathway to another is important.

The factors that prevent at risk children from developing any form of psychopathology are termed protective factors. Competent role models, positive stable relationships with care givers, positive peer relationships, positive ethnic identity and an easy temperament are all deemed to be important protective factors (Kerig, Ludlow & Werner, 2012).

Rutter (1990) proposed that instead on listing protective factors we look at the process behind these mechanisms. He proposed four protective mechanisms:

1 Reduction of risk of impact
2 Reduction of negative chain events
3 Promotion of self-efficacy
4 Increase in coping skills and opening of opportunities

Reduction of risk of impact suggests that some variables are able to intervene. For example, negative peer influences can be a powerful pull for a child towards delinquency. However, good relationships with parents who can monitor their behaviour and steer them to more positive role models will reduce this risk. The second mechanism, *reduction of negative chain events*, focuses on effects through relationships with other variables and the effects of vicious cycles. For example, a child with an easy-going temperament is less likely to be the target of a parent's anger and stress and will consequently show less behaviour problems, further decreasing parent's anger and stress. The third mechanism, factors that *promote self-esteem and self-efficacy* help children to feel they are able to cope with challenges in life. The final one, *opening of opportunities*, refers to children's opportunities to take advantage of turning points in life, for example a child who is bought up in extreme poverty studies hard at school in order to secure a better future.

👁 Diagnosis

Psychopathology is usually diagnosed with the help of the *Diagnostic and Statistical Manual of Mental Disorders* (DSM). This is a manual used by psychiatrists and GPs to help them decide which diagnosis a person experiencing mental distress should receive. The DSM was designed in order to try to standardise diagnostic practices such that, for example, a diagnosis of 'anxiety' would mean similar things to different practitioners. The DSM was first published in 1952 and lists different categories of psychopathology (mental disorders) alongside the criteria used to diagnose them. The criteria is determined and published by the American Psychiatric Association. There have been five revisions since it was first published, the most recent being DSM-5 in May 2013. The DSM-5 defines 17 categories of disorders, including neurodevelopmental disorders, schizophrenia spectrum and other psychotic disorders, anxiety disorders, depressive disorders and substance-related and addictive behaviours.

The World Health Organisation's *International Classification of Diseases* (ICD) is another classification tool and is largely used in the UK and Europe as an equivalent to the DSM. The most recent version ICD-11 was published in May 2013 and has the same categories as the DSM-5. Both the DSM and ICD are careful to state that it is the disorders, not individuals that are being classified.

The purpose of diagnosis

The purpose of a classification system is **differential diagnosis** – deciding which disorder best captures the symptoms of the disorder and which can be ruled out. This helps to dictate the best course of treatment available, such that, for example, an inattentive child showing signs of attention deficit hyperactivity disorder (ADHD) will be prescribed a different treatment and support programme compared to a child who shows attention problems due to severe anxiety. However, it is important to note that the problems of children very rarely fit neatly into one clear diagnostic category. Disorders in children are very often co-morbid, that is, they occur together. Consequently, children may receive multiple diagnoses rather than a single label. The clinical practitioner also uses the child's developmental history to establish the severity of the symptoms. The developmental period the child is in and the behaviours displayed will also be used to checklist the psychopathology most likely to be present.

Classification systems also allow for the development of epidemiological information about the incidence (risk of developing a disorder within a specific time frame) and prevalence (frequency at which a given behaviour occurs in a population at a given time) of various problems. This information is important in helping to identify risk factors and important milestones in developing different conditions. Common problems have been identified at critical age points. For example, early childhood is often linked to sleeping and toileting problems and is also the time frame in which learning disabilities and pervasive developmental disorders are more identifiable. In contrast, middle childhood is associated with conduct disorder, ADHD, anxiety problems and somatic complaints.

Finally, adolescence represents the period where drug abuse, depression, eating disorders and schizophrenia are more likely to be diagnosed (Carr, 2006).

Classification systems also provide a common language through which clinicians and researchers communicate with each other. If the diagnosis of ADHD is the same across all conditions it allows crucial information to be gained from studying children with ADHD, such as early risk factors and possible genetic and environmental causes.

We end this chapter by considering three developmental psycho-pathologies, autism spectrum disorders (ASD), anxiety and depression. Each of the three disorders is primarily identifiable at three of the critical time periods, ASD with early childhood, anxiety with middle childhood and depression with adolescence. ASD has largely been considered in line with the medical model due to a strong link to genetic factors.

As well as providing a brief summary to all three conditions, examples of different factors that affect the development of the disorders as well as risk and resilience are also considered.

Autism spectrum disorders

We start with ASD which is considered an unknown genetic disorder. Children with ASD are characterised by a triad of behaviour deficits: problems in communication, socialisation and imagination. Communication deficits include responding inappropriately in conversations and misleading nonverbal interactions and difficulty building relationships with others (DSM-5, APA 2013). In addition, people with ASD may be overly dependent on routines, highly sensitive to changes in their environment and/or focusing intently on inappropriate items. The symptoms of ASD will fall on a continuum, with some individuals showing mild symptoms and other having severe symptoms. Children are usually expected to show signs in early childhood, typically before the age of three, although they may be diagnosed at a later age.

There is a significant sex difference in the incidence of autism. On average across studies, boys outnumber girls at a ratio of four to one, a ratio that has not changed significantly from the time of Kanner's first diagnosis of autism (Fombonne, 1999). However, the ratios change when we look at autism in children with varying levels of cognitive ability: boys predominate less at the lower end of the IQ range. For example, in a large-scale study conducted in the UK, Wing (1991) found that at the lowest IQ levels, the ratio of boys to girls was two to one, whereas at the highest levels it was 15 to 1.The high incidence of autism found in males has led to the development of an idea first postulated by Hans Asperger (1944) who said 'that autistic personality is an extreme variant of male intelligence' Today this is more commonly referred to as the 'Extreme Male Brain' theory of autism' (Baron-Cohen, 2002) and implies that autism is resultant of over-developed 'male' characteristics. Happé, Briskman and Frith (2001) have also given more weight to this theory by demonstrating characteristics associated with autism to be more common in first-degree male relatives (brother, fathers). Whilst gender is a risk factor of autism, IQ and having a relative with autistic traits can both be seen vulnerabilities.

The biological context

In recent years, a number of environmental factors have been posited to play a causal role in autism. One of these involves birth complications. However, recent investigations have found birth complications to be either minor or no greater than those found in nonautistic infants with congenital anomalies. A second proposed environmental factor was congenital rubella. Initial studies suggested that rubella in pregnant mothers increased the incidence of autism in their infants. However, further research indicated that both the clinical description and the course of the children's disturbance were atypical; for example, such children tended to outgrow their presumed autism. Another alarming suggestion was that the combined measles, mumps, and rubella vaccine was a culprit. Because the media subsequently gave equal coverage to opposing views surrounding the link between the MMR vaccine and autism, parents understandably thought this meant that the scientific evidence for and against a link with autism was equally weighted. However, investigators have assessed the association between the incidence of autism and the introduction of the vaccine in several different countries and at several different time points and, to date, have found no discernable pattern (de los Reyes, 2010).

Genetic factors

There is little doubt that genetics plays an etiological role in autism. Although it is rare for parents to have two children with autism, the risk of having a second child with the disorder is 15–30 times higher for parents with an autistic child versus those with a typically developing youngster (Rutter, 2000; 2011).

As is always the case, the most convincing genetic data come from comparing monozygotic (MZ) with dizygotic (DZ) twins, one of whom has autism. General population twin studies yield concordance rates ranging from 36% to 91% for the MZ twins and from 0% to 5% for DZ twins. Further evidence for a strong genetic component in autism comes from the finding that the nonautistic MZ twins have some autistic characteristics but to a lesser degree, termed the 'broader autism phenotype'. Characteristics of the phenotype include some type of cognitive deficit, usually involving language delay, and persistent social impairment. Only 8% of the MZ co-twins were without such cognitive or social disorders compared with 90% of the DZ pairs. These studies suggest that the autistic phenotype extends well beyond the traditional diagnosis, involving characteristics similar to autism but markedly different in degree.

The intrapersonal context

Attachment

A core feature of autism is the lack of affectionate ties to caregivers, it stands to reason therefore that a fundamental disorder of attachment might lie at the heart of ASD. Indeed, there are qualitative differences between autistic and typically developing children in regard to attachment. In autistic children attachment-related behaviours are not accompanied by the same kind of emotional pleasure and reciprocity as they are in typically developing children. Behaviourally, attachment in children with autism is interspersed with characteristic repetitive motor movements such as hand-flapping, rocking and spinning. Their attachment-related behaviour is also more variable over time than it is in other children (Dissanayake, 2001).

Emotional development

A number of characteristic deficits in the area of emotional development point to this as a potential key to the mystery of autism. Children with autism, in contrast to typically developing children or those with mental retardation, have difficulty decoding the basic emotions as they are displayed on the human face (Baron-Cohen, Wheelwright, Hill, Raste & Plumb, 2001). Further, detailed studies of gaze patterns show that even individuals with autism who can discern emotional expressions do not look at faces in the same way that others do.

Infants with ASDs tend to be less attentive to people – especially their faces – and many other social cues in their environment (Dawson et al., 2004; Swettenham et al., 1998). The lack of interest in faces appears to be peculiar to disorders in the autistic spectrum, in that it sets apart these children not only from typically developing children but also from children with other developmental deficits.

Joint attention

Another feature of autism that has been proposed as the core of the disorder is a deficit in shared or joint attention. The typically developing 6–9-month-old will look between an object and the caretaker, as if to say, 'Look what I am looking at'. This is called 'referential looking'. Toward the end of the first year of life, the infant starts using referential gestures, such as pointing to an object when a caregiver is present or holding an object up for the caregiver to see. Rather than attending to the object alone, the infant now tries to attract the adult's attention so that the interest can be shared. In children with autism, shared attention behaviours are deficient or even absent (Osterling, Dawson, Munson, 2002).

Language development

Autistic speech tends to be echolalic, literal and lacking in prosody. We also know that there is great variation, ranging from mutism (particularly in autistic children with lower IQ scores) to speech that simply comes across as 'odd' in content.

Cognitive development

Children with ASD vary widely in performance of intelligence measurement tests, with scores ranging from in the average to the severely intellectually disabled range. Even when intelligence is intact, children in the autistic spectrum tend to show a particular pattern of scores that is consistent across different ability levels. Generally, children with autism score low on tests that assess their social reasoning. In contrast, children with autism perform best on tasks that assess reasoning about concrete objects, such as on the Block Design subtest, which requires children to solve a visual puzzle (Frith, 2003).

Children in the autistic spectrum also have difficulties in the area of executive functions involving planning, organisation, self-monitoring and cognitive flexibility.

One of the most profound cognitive deficits in children with ASDs – and one that some experts believe underlies and integrates all the others we have described – is a poor development of theory of mind. A key element for successful interaction in social situations is the understanding of other people's intentions, emotions and actions. Throughout childhood, an understanding of ToM is fundamental to skilled communication and social interaction, especially in complex situations including sarcasm, deception and humour (e.g., Harris, 2006).

◉ Anxiety disorders

Anxiety as an emotion is normative and serves a purpose in development. However when it goes awry and become debilitating and affects functioning in everyday life it is then considered a psychopathology. Anxiety disorders include among others generalised anxiety disorder, when everyday actions or requirements become a source of persistent but non-specific fear or worry, phobias of a specific situation, panic disorders, post-traumatic stress disorders or extreme separation anxiety (separation anxiety disorder).

Biological context

There is a lot of evidence to suggest that there exists a genetic risk element in developing an anxiety disorder (Gordon & Hen, 2004). For example, monozygotic twins have the highest chance of developing anxiety disorder compared to other siblings (Eley et al., 2006). A temperament variable of behaviour inhibition is also likely to increase the chance of children developing anxiety, particularly fear of social situations and specific phobias (Rothbart & Bates, 2006).

Family context

Infants with insecure attachment responses also display more fearful behaviour when exploring a strange situation than infants with secure attachment responses. Children with insecure ambivalent and insecure disorganised attachment patterns are thought to be particularly at risk from anxiety disorders, by as much as 100% (Manassis, 2001).

Individual context

Both cognitive biases and emotion regulation deficits have been shown to underlie anxiety. Information-processing biases include a selective attention to threatening information and also the interpretation of ambiguous stimuli as threatening. Unrealistic cognitive biases are also in evidence, such that those with anxiety disorders may tend to perceive the world as a dangerous place and perceive themselves as incompetent to deal with threats. They believe themselves unable to control threatening situations.

Skinner's operant conditioning model has been linked to the precipitation and development of anxiety. Whether through direct experience or observation, respondent conditioning produces in the child the expectation that a previously neutral stimulus will result in a negative consequent. An example is the anxious girl who approaches peers on the playground in an awkward manner and finds her bids to play are accordingly rejected. She may then view other social encounters as negative and avoid them. However positive prior learning may also act as protective factor against anxiety. For example, a child who has had many good experiences with dogs, but is then bitten by one may not develop a fear.

Piaget's cognitive schemata are also important to mention, as these schemata, that the child build-up of their knowledge of the world, may be attributed to distorted cognitive biases evidence in anxiety.

Whilst cognitive biases, avoidance of feared stimuli and poor emotional regulation intensify anxiety, so can over-protectiveness from the parents. Parents may act to protect their child but in doing so may reduce the child's exposure to positive experiences of dealing with fearful situations or anxious thoughts, thus reducing the child's ability to develop a more balanced cognitive and emotional model.

◉ Depression

Feeling 'down' or 'having the blues' is both common and normative. Depression as a syndrome includes symptoms that co-occur including feelings of sadness, loneliness and worry. Depression as a disorder (clinical depression) refers to profound levels of symptoms over a fixed duration. Whilst depression can emerge in childhood, during the transition to adolescence is when prevalence of the disorder increases dramatically.

The biological context

Children and adolescents who have family members with depression are at a higher risk of also developing depression, with a genetic component of about 20–45%.

Individual context

Insecure attachment styles have been found to relate to depression. Children who internalise an image of themselves as unworthy and others as unloving are more vulnerable to the development of the cognitive, emotional and biological processes of depression (Blatt & Homann, 1992).

Cognitive biases

Piaget's schema is again important to consider when we talk about depression. Children who develop depression have a cognitive triad (Beck, 2002): feelings of worthlessness, feelings of helplessness and feelings of hopelessness. These negative schemata affect not only the child's present state of mind but also the child's future orientation toward the world. Another cognitive style is rumination, when one dwells on negative thoughts and feelings. Females are thought to ruminate more often than males, which is a possible explanation for the fact that depression is more prevalent in females during adolescence.

Family context

An emotionally aversive family environment predicts the development of depression in children and adolescents (Harkness & Lumley, 2008). Families of depressed children report experiencing more acute and chronic stressors than do others. Here some of the social learning models of psychology are important to acknowledge.

Many factors are thought to increase and/or maintain levels of depression. The cultural context has been found to be a risk factor of depression; low household income and lack of parental educational have been found to contribute to high levels of depression. Stressful events in life are thought to lead to the development of negative cognitive styles. In contrast, maintaining contact with friends and a good social network is thought to act as a buffer to individuals at risk from depression.

Glossary

anal stage Freudian theoretical second stage of development in which the anus is the main zone of gratification. A failure to transfer the libido to the next stage will result in an anal-stage fixation, so the person may have a compulsive personality, focused either on excessive order or very disorganised.

attachment A concept introduced by John Bowlby which refers to the relationship an infant establishes with an adult, usually the main caregiver.

autonomous morality A moral developmental stage in which the person considers the intentions behind an action, and not only its consequence, to evaluate whether the action is right or wrong. At this stage the person understands that norms and rules can change depending on the circumstances.

blank slate (*tabula rasa*) A theoretical stage that suggests individuals are born without mental content, and that all the knowledge is acquired through perception and experience.

classical conditioning Learning based on the relationship between a conditioned stimulus (CS, e.g., a ringtone) when it is matched to an unconditional stimulus (US, e.g., food), resulting in an unconditional response (UR, e.g., salivation). After learning, the CS (bell) produces the now conditioned response (CR, salivation) without the presence of the UC (food).

cognitive revolution Academic and intellectual movement in some 'cognitive sciences' like psychology and linguistics. It was a movement that proposed that researchers should investigate the cognitive mechanisms responsible for behaviour, and not just behaviour itself as behaviourism proposed.

conservation tasks The understanding that even if appearance of something changes the quantity will stay the same. Can relate to mass, numbers and volume

differential diagnosis A systematic method to diagnose a disorder or a disease that does not have specific causes, or when different equally possible explanations can account for an accurate diagnosis

empirical observation Method in which knowledge is acquired by observation of some phenomena or experimentation. It is based on observed evidence that confirms or refutes a hypothesis about the phenomena.

etiology Refers to the study of causes. In developmental psychopathology it refer to the study of causes of a disorder or a disease.

expiatory punishment The belief that a punishment should correspond to the wrongness of the behaviour. The worse the action, the worse the punishment that should follow the behaviour.

false belief tasks A test used to measure whether a person has a 'false belief', the ability to recognise that others may have a different view of the world as the person. A false belief task usually consist in asking a person to take the perspective of others and respond to some simple questions. The person can then respond based on his or her own beliefs (not passing the task) or as the other person (passing the task).

fixation In Freudian terms, is a situation in which the libido is not appropriately transferred from one erogenous zone to another, affecting the development and personality of the person. Freud proposed that the libido is transferred from one zone to another in stages (oral, anal, phallic, latency and genital).

genital stage Freudian theoretical fifth stage of development. Although the genitalia is the main zone of gratification, it is different to the phallic stage as the ego of the person is already established, leading to a search of gratification with other adults in the form of romantic relationships, friendships and adult responsibilities.

immanent justice The belief that negative behaviour will, somehow, be punished. Even if the direct relationship between a negative action and negative consequences does not exist, a child thinks that a negative experience is a punishment for previous misconducts.

innate skills Characteristics or skills that are present when the person is born. These characteristics or skills are not learned through experience.

latency period Freudian theoretical fourth stage of development in which the libido is latent and the person focuses the energy on external social activities, such as school and play.

moral domain theory Proposal of Turiel that suggests that children acquire knowledge about the 'moral domain', that is, ideas about fairness, welfare, justice and rights. According to Turiel, children use these concepts to evaluate whether an action is morally right, regardless of what the rules state.

moral heteronomy A moral developmental stage in which children consider that laws and rules are set and can not be changed. The consequences associated to an action determine whether the action is right or wrong, not the intention of the person.

nature–nurture debate Academic disagreement about the relative importance and causes of skills and abilities. The 'nature' side suggests that physical and behavioural traits are strongly innate, whereas the 'nurture' side suggests that physical and behavioural skills are strongly affected by learning and experience.

operant conditioning Learning where behaviour is modified through the use of positive and negative reinforcement.

oral stage Freudian theoretical first stage of development in which the mouth is the main zone of gratification. A failure to transfer the libido to the next stage will result in an oral-stage fixation, so the person may have an immature or manipulative personality.

phallic stage Freudian theoretical third stage of development in which the genitalia is the main zone of gratification. The Oedipus complex (and for some other psychoanalysts, the Electra complex in girls) is a consequence of this stage. A phallic-stage fixation may result in sexual deviances, such as being overindulgent or very repressed.

pleasure principle A Freudian term that refers to the instinctual search for gratification and pleasure, and the avoidance of pain or suffering. It is the main driving force of the id.

questionnaire techniques A research technique that relies on asking a series of questions to respondents in order to gather information. Questionnaires are often used to gather a relative large amount of information from a large number of respondents, asking the same questions to all of them.

reality principle A Freudian term that refers to the capacity to evaluate and respond to the external based on cultural and social demands. The reality principle is a counterpart of the pleasure principle and the driving force of the ego, which defers the instant demands of the id into socially and culturally acceptable manners.

theory of mind The cognitive capacity to attribute mental states, beliefs, desires, intentions and knowledge to self and others.

References

Adler, A. (1927). *Understanding Human Nature*. Oxford: Greenberg.

Ainsworth, M. D. S., Blehar, M. C., Waters, E. & Wall, S. (1978). *Patterns of Attachment: A Psychological Study of the Strange Situation*. Hillsdale, NJ: Lawrence Erlbaum.

Aitchison, J. (1996). *The Seeds of Speech – Language Origin and Evolution*. Cambridge: Cambridge University Press.

Ambridge, B. & Lieven, E. V. (2011). *Child Language Acquisition: Contrasting Theoretical Approaches*. Cambridge: Cambridge University Press.

American Psychiatric Association (2013). *Diagnostic and Statistical Manual of Mental Disorders*, 5th edn. Washington, DC: American Psychiatric Association.

Aries, P. (1962). *Centuries of Childhood*. New York: Vintage.

Asperger, H. (1944). Die 'autistischen Psychopathen' im Kindesalter. *Archiv für Psychiatrie und Nervenkrankheiten*, *117*, 76–136.

Atkinson, I. A. (1996). Introductions of wildlife as a cause of species extinctions. *Wildlife Biology*, *2*(3), 135–141.

Bafunno, D. & Camodeca, M. (2013). Shame and guilt development in preschoolers: The role of context, audience and individual characteristics. *European Journal of Developmental Psychology*, *10*(2), 128–143. doi: 10.1080/17405629.2013.765796.

Bagwell, C. L., Newcomb, A. F. & Bukowski, W. M. (1998). Preadolescent friendship and peer rejection as predictors of adult adjustment. *Child Development*, *69*(1), 140–153. doi: 10.1111/j.1467-8624.1998.tb06139.x.

Baillargeon, R. (1995). A model of physical reasoning in infancy. *Advances in Infancy Research*, *9*, 305–371.

Baillargeon, R., Spelke, E. S. & Wasserman, S. (1985). Object permanence in five-month-old infants. *Cognition*, *20*(3), 191–208. doi: org/10.1016/0010-0277(85)90008-3.

Baker, J., Horton, S., Robertson-Wilson, J. & Wall, M. (2003). Nurturing sport expertise: Factors influencing the development of elite athlete. *Journal of Sports Science and Medicine*, *2*(1), 1–9.

Bandura, A. (1977). Self-efficacy: Toward a unifying theory of behavioral change. *Psychological Review*, *84*(2), 191–215. doi: 10.1037/0033-295X.84.2.191.

Bandura. A. (1986). *Social Foundations of Thought and Action: A Social Cognitive Theory*. Englewood Cliffs, NJ: Prentice-Hall.

Bandura, A., Ross, D. & Ross, S. A. (1961). Transmission of aggression through imitation of aggressive models. *The Journal of Abnormal and Social Psychology*, *63*(3), 575–582. doi: 10.1037/h0045925.

Baron-Cohen, S. (2002). The extreme male brain theory of autism. *Trends in Cognitive Sciences*, *6*(6), 248–254. doi: org/10.1016/S1364-6613(02)01904-6.

Baron-Cohen, S., Leslie, A. M. & Frith, U. (1985). Does the autistic child have a 'theory of mind'? *Cognition*, *21*(1), 37–46. doi: org/10.1016/0010-0277(85)90022-8.

Baron-Cohen, S., Wheelwright, S., Hill, J., Raste, Y. & Plumb, I. (2001). The 'Reading the mind in the eyes' test revised version: A study with normal adults, and adults with Asperger syndrome or high-functioning autism. *Journal of Child Psychology and Psychiatry*, *42*(2), 241–251. doi: 10.1111/1469-7610.00715.

Barr, R., Dowden, A. & Hayne, H. (1996). Developmental changes in deferred imitation by 6- to 24-month-old infants. *Infant Behavior and Development*, *19*(2), 159–170.

Barrett, K. C. (1995). A functionalist approach to shame and guilt. In J. P. Tangney & K. W. Fischer (Eds), *Self-conscious Emotions: The Psychology of Shame, Guilt, Embarrassment, and Pride* (pp. 25–63). New York: Guilford Press.

Bartsch, K. & Wellman, H. M. (1995). *Children Talk about the Mind*. Oxford & New York: Oxford University Press.

Bates, E. (1993). Modularity, domain specificity and the development of language. *Discussions in Neuroscience*, *10*(1), 136–148.

Beck, A. T. (2002). Cognitive models of depression. *Clinical Advances in Cognitive Psychotherapy: Theory and Application, 14*, 29–61.

Belmonte, M. K. & Bourgeron, T. (2006). Fragile X syndrome and autism at the intersection of genetic and neural networks. *Nature Neuroscience, 9*(10), 1221–1225. doi: 10.1038/nn1765.

Benoit, D. (2004). Infant-parent attachment: Definition, types, antecedents, measurement and outcome. *Paediatrics & Child Health, 9*(8), 541.

Berk, L. E. (2011). *Development Through the Lifespan* (6th edn) Boston: Pearson.

Berman, C. M., Rasmussen, K. L. R. & Suomi, S. J. (1993). Reproductive consequences of maternal care patterns during estrus among free-ranging rhesus monkeys. *Behavioral Ecology and Sociobiology, 32*(6), 391–399.

Blake, B. & Pope, T. (2008). Developmental psychology: Incorporating Piaget's and Vygotsky's theories in classrooms. *Journal of Cross-Disciplinary Perspectives in Education, 1*(10), 59–67.

Blatt, S. J. & Homann, E. (1992). Parent-child interaction in the etiology of dependent and self-critical depression. *Clinical Psychology Review, 12*(1), 47–91. doi: org/10.1016/0272-7358(92)90070-O.

Bonner, W. N. (1980). *Whales.* Poole: Blandford Press.

Bornstein, M. H. (1989). Sensitive periods in development: Structural characteristics and causal interpretations. *Psychological Bulletin, 105*(2), 179–197. doi: 10.1037/0033-2909.105.2.179.

Bouchard, T. J., Lykken, D. T., McGue, M., Segal, N. L. & Tellegen, A. (1990). Sources of human psychological differences: The Minnesota study of twins reared apart. *Science, 250*(4978), 223–228. doi:10.1126/science.2218526.

Bowlby, J. (1951). *Maternal Care and Mental Health* (p. 157). Geneva: World Health Organization.

Bowlby, J. (1958). The nature of a child's tie to his mother. *International Journal of Psycho-Analysis, 39*, 350–373.

Bowlby, J. (1969). *Attachment and Loss: Vol. 1, Attachment.* London: Random House.

Bradshaw, C. P., Goldweber, A. & Garbarino, J. (2013). Linking social-environmental risk factors with aggression in suburban adolescents: The role of social-cognitive mediators. *Psychology in the Schools, 50*(5), 433–450. doi: 10.1002/pits.21690.

Brainerd, C. J. (1978). *Piaget's Theory of Intelligence*. Englewood Cliffs, NJ: Prentice-Hall.

Brandler, W. M. & Paracchini, S. (2014). The genetic relationship between handedness and neurodevelopmental disorders. *Trends in Molecular Medicine, 20*(2), doi: org/10.1016/j.molmed.2013.10.008.

Bremner, J. D. (1999). Does stress damage the brain. *Biological Psychiatry, 45*, 797–805.

Bretherton, I. (1985). Attachment theory: Retrospect and prospect. *Monographs of the Society for Research in Child Development, 50*(1/2), 3–35. doi: 10.2307/3333824.

Brody, L. R. (1999). *Gender, Emotion and the Family*. Cambridge, MA: Harvard University Press.

Brody, L. R. (2000). The socialization of gender differences in emotional expression: Display rules, infant temperament, and differentiation. In A. H. Fischer (Ed.) *Gender and Emotion: Social Psychological Perspectives* (pp. 24–47). Cambridge: Cambridge University Press.

Brody, L. R. & Hall, J. A. (2000). Gender, emotion, and expression. In M. Lewis & J. M. Haviland (Eds), *Handbook of Emotions*, 2nd edn (pp. 338–349). New York: Guilford.

Bronfenbrenner, U. (1974). Is early intervention effective? *Early Childhood Education Journal, 2*(2), 14–18. doi: 10.1007/BF02353057.

Bronfenbrenner, U. (1979). *The Ecology of Human Development*. Cambridge, MA: Harvard University Press.

Bronfenbrenner, U. & Morris, P. A. (1998). The ecology of developmental processes. In R. Lerner (Vol. ed.) *Handbook of Child Psychology: Theoretical Models of Human Development*. 5th edn (vol. 1, pp. 993–1028). New York: John Wiley.

Brooks-Gunn, J. (1982). Developmental processes in the experience of menarche. In A. Baum & J. E. Singer (Eds), *Issues in Child Health and Adolescent Health: Handbook of Psychology and Health, Vol. 2* (pp. 117–147). Hillsdale, NJ: Lawrence Erlbaum.

Brooks-Gunn, J. & Lewis, M. (1979). 'Why mama and papa?' The development of social labels. *Child Development, 50*, 1203–1206.

Brooks-Gunn, J., & Ruble, D. N. (2013). Developmental processes in the experience of menarche. *Issues in Child Health and Adolescent Health: Handbook of Psychology and Health, 2*, 117-147.

Brooker, R. J., Buss, K. A., Lemery-Chalfant, K., Aksan, N., Davidson, R. J. & Goldsmith, H. H. (2013). The development of stranger fear in infancy and toddlerhood: Normative development, individual differences, antecedents, and outcomes. *Developmental Science*, *16*(6), 864–878. doi: 10.1111/desc.12058.

Brown, A. L. & Palincsar, A. S. (1989). Guided, cooperative learning and individual knowledge acquisition. In L. B. Resnick (Ed.) *Knowing, Learning, and Instruction: Essays in Honor of Robert Glaser* (pp. 393–451). Hillsdale, NJ: Lawrence Erlbaum.

Bruner, J. S. (1983). *In Search of Mind: Essays in Autobiography*. New York: Harper & Row.

Budhall, R. S. (1998). *The Socially Isolated Child at School*. Unpublished DEd thesis. Pretoria: University of South Africa.

Burkhardt, R. W. (2005). *Patterns of Behavior: Konrad Lorenz, Niko Tinbergen, and the Founding of Ethology*. Chicago: University of Chicago Press.

Butterfield, F. C. & Siperstein, G. M. (1972). Influence of contingent auditory stimulation upon non nutritional suckle. In J. Bosma (Ed.), *Oral Sensation and Perception: In the Mouth of an Infant* (pp. 313–314). Springfield, IL: Thomas.

Carr, A. (2006). *The Handbook of Child and Adolescent Clinical Psychology: A Contextual Approach*. London: Routledge.

Casey, R. J. & Fuller, L. L. (1994). Maternal regulation of children's emotions. *Journal of Nonverbal Behavior*, *18*(1), 57–89.

Cassibba, R., van IJzendoorn, M. H. & Coppola, G. (2012). Emotional availability and attachment across generations: Variations in patterns associated with infant health risk status. *Child: Care, Health and Development*, *38*(4), 538–544. doi: 10.1111/j.1365-2214.2011.01274.x.

Chomsky, C. (1965). *The Acquisition of Language from Five to Ten*. Cambridge, MA: MIT Press.

Cicchetti, D. (2014). Illustrative developmental psychopathology perspectives on precursors and pathways to personality disorder: Commentary on the special issue. *Journal of Personality Disorders*, *28*(1), 172–179. doi: 10.1521/pedi.2014.28.1.172.

Cohen, N. J., Farnia, F. & Im-Bolter, N. (2013). Higher order language competence and adolescent mental health. *Journal of Child Psychology and Psychiatry*, *54*(7), 733–744. doi: 0.1111/jcpp.12060.

Coie, J. D. & Dodge, K. A. (1983). Continuities and changes in children's social status: A five-year longitudinal study. *Merrill-Palmer Quarterly (1982–)*, *29*(3), 261–282.

Colby, A., Kohlberg, L., Gibbs, J., Lieberman, M., Fischer, K. & Saltzstein, H. D. (1983). A longitudinal study of moral judgment. *Monographs of the Society for Research in Child Development*, *48*(1/2), 1–124.

Cole, P. M. (1986). Children's spontaneous control of facial expression. *Child Development*, *57*(6), 1309–1321.

Cornell, A. H. & Frick, P. J. (2007). The moderating affects of parenting styles in the association between behavioral inhibition and parent-reported guilt and empathy in preschool children. *Journal of Clinical Child and Adolescent Psychology*, *36*, 305–318. doi: 0.1080/15374410701444181.

Craissati, J., McClurg, G. & Browne, K. (2002). The parental bonding experiences of sex offenders: A comparison between child molesters and rapists. *Child Abuse & Neglect*, *26*(9), 909–921. doi: org/10.1016/S0145-2134(02)00361-7.

Crick, N. R. & Dodge, K. A. (1994). A review and reformulation of social information-processing mechanisms in children's social adjustment. *Psychological Bulletin*, *115*(1), 74–101. doi: 10.1037/0033-2909.115.1.74.

Curtiss, S. (1977). Genie: A psycholinguistic study of a modern-day 'Wild Child'. *New York: Academic Press*, *1*, 131–157.

Daniels, H. (2001). *Vygotsky and Pedagogy*. New York: Routledge/Falmer.

Davis, K. M., Gagnier, K. R., Moore, T. E. & Todorow, M. (2013). Cognitive aspects of fetal alcohol spectrum disorder. *Wiley Interdisciplinary Reviews: Cognitive Science*, *4*(1), 81–92. doi: 10.1002/wcs.1202.

Dawson, G., Toth, K., Abbott, R., Osterling, J., Munson, J., Estes, A. & Liaw, J. (2004). Early social attention impairments in autism: Social orienting, joint attention, and attention to distress. *Developmental Psychology*, *40*(2), 271–283. doi: 10.1037/0012-1649.40.2.271.

de los Reyes, E. C. (2010). Autism and immunizations: Separating fact from fiction. *Archives of Neurology*, *67*(4), 490. doi: 10.1001/archneurol.2010.57.

Deary, I. J. (2000). *Looking Down on Human Intelligence: From Psychometrics to the Brain*. Oxford: Oxford University Press.

DeCasper, A. J. & Fifer, W. P. (1980). Of human bonding: Newborns prefer their mothers' voices. *Science*, *208*(4448), 1174–1176. doi: *10.1126/science.7375928*.

Dehaene-Lambertz, G., Hertz-Pannier, L., Dubois, J., Mériaux, S., Roche, A., Sigman, M. & Dehaene, S. (2006). Functional organization of perisylvian activation during presentation of sentences in preverbal infants. *Proceedings of the National Academy of Sciences*, *103*(38), 14240–14245.

Diamond, J. (1991). *The Rise and Fall of the Third Chimpanzee*. London, Sydney, Auckland, Johannesburg: Radius, Random Century.

Dickinson, D. K. & Tabors, P. O. (1991). Early literacy: Linkages between home, school and literacy achievement at age five. *Journal of Research in Childhood Education*, 6(1), 30–46. doi: 10.1080/02568549109594820.

Dissanayake, E. (2001). Becoming Homo Aestheticus: Sources of aesthetic imagination in mother-infant interactions. *Substance*, 30(1), 85–103. doi: 10.1353/sub.2001.0005.

Dubas, J. S., Graber, J. A. & Petersen, A. C. (1991). A longitudinal investigation of adolescents' changing perceptions of pubertal timing. *Developmental Psychology*, 27(4), 580–586. doi: 10.1037/0012-1649.27.4.580.

Duderstadt, K. (2013). *Pediatric Physical Examination: An Illustrated Handbook*, 2nd edn. St Louis, MO: Elsevier Health Sciences.

Dunn, J., Bretherton, I. & Munn, P. (1987). Conversations about feeling states between mothers and their young children. *Developmental Psychology*, 23(1), 132–139. doi: 10.1037/0012-1649.23.1.132.

Eisenberg, N. (2000). Emotion, regulation, and moral development. *Annual Review of Psychology*, 51(1), 665–697.

Eisenberg, N. & Fabes, R. A. (1994). Mothers' reactions to children's negative emotions: Relations to children's temperament and anger behavior. *Merrill-Palmer Quarterly (1982–)*, 40(1), 138–156.

Eisenberg, N., Cumberland, A. & Spinrad, T. L. (1998). Parental socialization of emotion. *Psychological Inquiry*, 9(4), 241–273.

Eisenberg, N., Fabes, R. A. & Murphy, B. C. (1996). Parents' reactions to children's negative emotions: Relations to children's social competence and comforting behavior. *Child Development*, 67(5), 2227–2247. doi: 10.1111/j.1467-8624.1996.tb01854.x.

Ekerman, C. O. & Stein, M. (1990). How imitation begets imitation and toddlers' generation of games. *Developmental Psychology*, 26, 370–378.

Ekman, P. & Friesen, W. V. (1978). *Facial Action Coding System: A Technique for the Measurement of Facial Movement*. Palo Alto, CA: Consulting Psychologists Press.

Elder Jr, G. H. (1995). The life course paradigm: Social change and individual development. In G. H. Elder Jr, P. Moen & K. Lüscher (Eds), *Examining Lives in Context: Perspectives on the Ecology of Human Development* (pp. 101–139). Washington, DC, US: American Psychological Association. doi: 10.1037/10176-003.

Elder, G. H. (1998). The life course as developmental theory. *Child Development*, *69*(1), 1–12. doi: 10.1111/j.1467-8624.1998.tb06128.x.

Eley, T. C., Bolton, D., O'Connor, T. G., Perrin, S., Smith, P., & Plomin, R. (2003). A twin study of anxiety-related behaviours in pre-school children. *Journal of Child Psychology and Psychiatry*, *44*(7), 945–960. doi.10.1111/1469-7610.00179.

Eliot, L. (2010). *What's Going on in There?: How the Brain and Mind Develop in the First Five Years of Life*. New York: Random House Digital, Inc.

Erikson, E. H. (1950). Growth and crises of the 'healthy personality'. In E. H. Erikson & M. J. E. Senn (Eds), *Symposium on the Healthy Personality* (pp. 91–146). Oxford: Josiah Macy, Jr. Foundation.

Erikson, E. H. (1963). *Childhood and Society* (Rev. edn) (pp. 159–256). New York: Norton.

Feiring, C., Lewis, M. & Starr, M. D. (1984). Indirect effects and infants' reaction to strangers. *Developmental Psychology*, *20*(3), 485–491. doi: 10.1037/0012-1649.20.3.485.

Field, T. (1984). Play behaviors of handicapped children who have friends. In T. Field, J. L. Roopnarine & M. Segal (Eds), *Friendships in Normal and Handicapped Children* (pp. 153–163). Norwood, NJ: Ablex.

Fischer, A. H. (1993). Sex differences in emotionality: Fact or stereotype? *Feminism & Psychology*, *3*(3), 303–318. doi: 10.1177/0959353593033002.

Fitch, W. T., Hauser, M. D. & Chomsky, N. (2005). The evolution of the language faculty: Clarifications and implications. *Cognition*, *97*(2), 179–210. doi: org/10.1016/j.cognition.2005.02.005.

Fivush, R. & Buckner, J. P. (2000). Gender, sadness, and depression: The development of emotional focus through gendered discourse. In A. H. Fischer (Ed.) *Gender and Emotion: Social Psychological Perspectives* (pp. 232–253). Cambridge: Cambridge University Press.

Fogel, A. (1993). *Developing through Relationships*. Chicago: University of Chicago Press.

Fombonne, E. (1999). The epidemiology of autism: A review. *Psychological Medicine*, *29*(4), 769–786.

Fonagy, P., Steele, H. & Steele, M. (1991). Maternal representations of attachment during pregnancy predict the organization of infant-mother attachment at one year of age. *Child Development*, *62*(5), 891–905. doi: 10.1111/j.1467-8624.1991.tb01578.x.

Fouts, R. & Mills, S. T. (1997). *Next of Kin: What Chimpanzees Have Taught Me about Who We Are.* New York: William Morrow.

Fowler, J. C. (2010). Review of handbook of evidence-based psychodynamic psychotherapy: Bridging the gap between science and practice. *Psychoanalytic Psychology, 27*(1), 94–98. doi: 10.1037/ a0018656.

Freud, S. (1920). *A General Introduction to Psychoanalysis.* New York: Horace Liveright.

Freud, S. (1923). Certain neurotic mechanisms in jealousy, paranoia and homosexuality. *International Journal of Psycho-Analysis, 4*, 1–10.

Freud, S. (1958). The disposition to obsessional neurosis, a contribution to the problem of the choice of neurosis. In *The Standard Edition of the Complete Psychological Works of Sigmund Freud, Vol. XII (1911–1913): The Case of Schreber, Papers on Technique and Other Works* (pp. 311–326). London: Hogarth Press.

Fritz, G. K. & McQuaid, E. L. (2000). Chronic medical conditions. In A. J. Sameroff, M. Lewis & S. M. Miller (Eds), *Handbook of Developmental Psychopathology*, 2nd edn (pp. 277–289). New York: Springer US.

Frith, C. (2003). What do imaging studies tell us about the neural basis of autism. In Novartis Foundation, *Autism: Neural Basis and Treatment Possibilities* (pp. 149–176). Chichester: Wiley.

Fromkin, V. & Rodman, R. (1998). *An Introduction to Language*, 6th edn. Fort Worth: Harcourt Brace.

Gallahue, D. L. (1993). Motor development and movement skill acquisition in early childhood education. In B. Spodek (Ed.) *Handbook of Research on the Education of Young Children* (pp. 24–41). London: Macmillan.

Gallahue, D. L. & Ozmun, J. C. (1989). *Understanding Motor Development: Infants, Children, Adolescents.* Indianapolis: Benchmark.

Gardner, R. A. & Gardner, B. T. (1969). Teaching sign language to a chimpanzee. *Science, 165*(3894), 664–672.

Ge, X., Conger, R. D. & Elder, G. H. (1996). Coming of age too early: Pubertal influences on girls' vulnerability to psychological distress. *Child Development, 67*(6), 3386–3400.

Gergely, G. & Watson, J. S. (1999). Early socio-emotional development: Contingency perception and the social-biofeedback model. In P. Rochat (Ed.) *Early Social Cognition: Understanding Others in the First Months of Life.* New Jersey: Lawrence Erlbaum.

Gibson, E. J. & Walk, R. D. (1960). *The 'Visual Cliff'*. Scientific American offprints. New York: WH Freeman.

Gilligan, C. (1982). *In a Different Voice: Psychological Theory and Women's Development*. Cambridge, MA: Harvard University Press.

Ginsburg, H. P. & Opper, S. (1988). *Piaget's Theory of Intellectual Development*. New Jersey: Prentice-Hall.

Gluck, J. P., Bell, J. B., & Pearson-Bish (2003). Confronting ethical issues in the use of animals in biomedical and behavioral research. In W. O'Donohue & K. Ferguson (Eds), *Handbook of Professional Ethics for Psychologists: Issues, Questions, and Controversies* (pp. 257–275). Thousand Oaks, CA: Sage.

Gopnik, A. & Wellman, H. M. (1994). The theory theory. In L. A. Hirschfeld & S. A. Gelman (Eds), *Mapping the Mind: Domain Specificity in Cognition and Culture* (pp. 257–293). New York: Cambridge University Press.

Gordon, J. A. & Hen, R. (2004). Genetic approaches to the study of anxiety. *Annual Review of Neuroscience, 27*, 193–222. doi. 0.1146/annurev.neuro.27.070203.144212.

Gustafsson, E., Levréro, F., Reby, D. & Mathevon, N. (2013). Fathers are just as good as mothers at recognizing the cries of their baby. *Nature Communications, 4*, 1698. doi: 10.1038/ncomms2713.

Hagerman, R. J. (2005). Fragile X syndrome. In S. B. Cassidy & J. E. Allanson (Eds), *Management of Genetic Syndromes*, 2nd edn (pp. 251–253). Hoboken, NJ: Wiley.

Haidt, J. (2003). The moral emotions. In R. J. Davidson, K. R. Scherer & H. H. Goldsmith (Eds), *Handbook of Affective Sciences* (pp. 852–870). Oxford: Oxford University Press.

Handwerker, H. O. (2007). From Descartes to fMRI: Pain theories and pain concepts. *Schmerz, 21*(4), 307–310, 312–317.

Happé, F., Briskman, J. & Frith, U. (2001). Exploring the cognitive phenotype of autism: Weak 'central coherence' in parents and siblings of children with autism: I. Experimental tests. *Journal of Child Psychology and Psychiatry, 42*(3), 299–307. doi: 10.1111/1469-7610.00723.

Harkness, K. L. & Lumley, M. N. (2008). Child abuse and neglect and the development of depression in children and adolescents. In J. R. Abela & B. L. Hankin (Eds), *Handbook of Depression in Children and Adolescents* (pp. 466–488). New York: Guilford.

Harlow, H. F. & Zimmermann, R. R. (1958). The development of affectional responses in infant monkeys. *Proceedings of the American Philosophical Society, 102*(5), 501–509.

Harris, J. R. (1998). *The Nurture Assumption: Why Children Turn Out the Way They Do*. New York: Free Press.

Harris, P. L. (1989). *Children and Emotion*. Oxford: Blackwell.

Harris, P. L. (2006). Social cognition. In D. Kuhn, R. S. Siegler, W. Damon & R. M. Lerner (Eds), *Handbook of Child Psychology: Vol. 2, Cognition, Perception, and Language*, 6th edn (pp. 811–858). Hoboken, NJ: Wiley.

Hassold, T. & Sherman, S. (2000). Down syndrome: Genetic recombination and the origin of the extra chromosome 21. *Clinical Genetics, 57*(2), 95–100. doi: 10.1034/j.1399-0004.2000.570201.x.

Haworth, C. M., Wright, M. J., Luciano, M., Martin, N. G., deGeus, E. J., van Beijsterveldt, C. E., Bartels, M., Posthuma, D., Boomsma, D. I., Davis, O. S., Kovas, Y., Corley, R. P., DeFries, J. C., Hewitt, J. K., Olson, R. K., Rhea, S. A., Wadsworth, S. J., Iacono, W. G., McGue, M., Thompson, L. A., Hart, S. A., Petrill, S. A., Lubinski, D. & Plomin, R. (2010). The heritability of general cognitive ability increases linearly from childhood to young adulthood. *Molecular Psychiatry, 15*, 1112–1120.

Hedeager, U. (1992). Is language unique to the human species? Columbia, pp. 1–12.

Hines, M. (2006). Prenatal testosterone and gender-related behaviour. *European Journal of Endocrinology, 155*(suppl. 1), 115–121. doi: 10.1530/eje.1.02236.

Hoare, C. H. (2002). *Erikson on Development in Adulthood: New Insights from the Unpublished Papers*. Oxford: Oxford University Press.

Hoffman, D. M. (2010). Risky investments: Parenting and the production of the 'resilient child'. *Health, Risk & Society, 12*(4), 385–394. doi: 10.1080/13698571003789716.

Irwin, D. M. & Moore, S. G. (1971). The young child's understanding of social justice. *Developmental Psychology, 5*(3), 406–410. doi: 10.1037/h0031614.

Isom, M. D. (1998). The social learning theory. Retrieved 18 September 2013. http://www.criminology.fsu.edu/crimtheory/bandura.htm.

Izard, C. E. (1994). Innate and universal facial expressions: Evidence from developmental and cross-cultural research. *Psychological Bulletin, 115*(2), 288–299. doi: 10.1037/0033-2909.115.2.288.

Izard, C. E. (2009). Emotion theory and research: Highlights, unanswered questions, and emerging issues. *Annual Review of Psychology, 60*, 1–25.

Jenkins, J. M. & Astington, J. W. (1996). Cognitive factors and family structure associated with theory of mind development in young children. *Developmental Psychology, 32*(1), 70–78. doi: 10.1037/0012-1649.32.1.70.

Jenvey, V. (2013). The utility of psychological theories in understanding the social development of contemporary children. Paper presented at 3rd Global Conference on Childhood, University of Oxford, Oxford, UK.

Johnson, J. S. & Newport, E. L. (1989). Critical period effects in second language learning: The influence of maturational state on the acquisition of English as a second language. *Cognitive Psychology*, *21*(1), 60–99. doi: org/10.1016/0010-0285(89)90003-0.

Jung, C. G. (1963). *Memories, Dreams, Reflections*, transl. by R. Winston & C. Winston. New York: Random House.

Kaye, K. (1982). *The Mental and Social Life of Babies*. Chicago: University of Chicago.

Keel, P. K., Fulkerson, J. A. & Leon, G. R. (1997). Disordered eating precursors in pre- and early adolescent girls and boys. *Journal of Youth and Adolescence*, *26*(2), 203–216. doi: 10.1023/A:1024504615742.

Keenan, T. & Evans, S. (2009). *An Introduction to Child Development*. Thousand Oaks, CA: Sage.

Kerig, P., Ludlow, A. K. & Werner, C. (2012). *Developmental Psychopathology*. Oxford: McGraw Hill.

Klinnert, M. D. (1984). The regulation of infant behavior by maternal facial expression. *Infant Behavior and Development*, *7*, 447–465.

Knafo, A., Zahn-Waxler, C., Van Hulle, C., Robinson, J. L. & Rhee, S. H. (2008). The developmental origins of a disposition toward empathy: Genetic and environmental contributions. *Emotion*, *8*(6), 737–752. doi: 10.1037/a0014179.

Koe, A. S., Salzberg, M. R., Morris, M. J., O'Brien, T. J. & Jones, N. C. (2014). Early life maternal separation stress augmentation of limbic epileptogenesis: The role of corticosterone and HPA axis programming. *Psychoneuroendocrinology*, *42*, 124–133.

Kohlberg, L. (1958). *The Development of Modes of Moral Thinking and Choice in the Years 10 to 16*. Chicago: University of Chicago.

Kohlberg, L. (1963). The development of children's orientations toward a moral order. *Human Development*, *6*(1–2), 11–33.

Kroll, J. & Egan, E. (2004). Psychiatry, moral worry, and the moral emotions. *Journal of Psychiatric Practice*, *10*(6), 352–360.

Kuhn, D. (1995). Microgenetic study of change: What has it told us? *Psychological Science*, *6*, 133–139.

Kurtines, W. & Greif, E. B. (1974). The development of moral thought: Review and evaluation of Kohlberg's approach. *Psychological Bulletin*, *81*(8), 453–470. doi: 10.1037/h0036879.

Ladd, G. W. (1990). Having friends, keeping friends, making friends, and being liked by peers in the classroom: Predictors of children's early school adjustment? *Child Development, 61*(4), 1081–1100. doi: 10.1111/j.1467-8624.1990.tb02843.x.

Lavelli, M., Pantoja, A. P., Hsu, H., Messinger, D. & Fogel, A. (2005). Using microgenetic designs to study change processes. In D. M. Teti (Ed.) *Handbook of Research Methods in Developmental Science* (pp. 40–65). Malden, MA: Blackwell.

Lazarus, R. S. (1991a). *Emotion and Adaptation*. Oxford: Oxford University Press.

Lazarus, R. S. (1991b). Progress on a cognitive-motivational-relational theory of emotion. *American Psychologist, 46*(8), 819–834. doi: 10.1037/0003-066X.46.8.819.

Lee, Y. & Styne, D. (2013). Influences on the onset and tempo of puberty in human beings and implications for adolescent psychological development. *Hormones and Behavior, 64*(2), 250–261.

Lempers, J. D., Flavell, E. R. & Flavell, J. H. (1977). The development in very young children of tacit knowledge concerning visual perception. *Genetic Psychology Monographs, 95*(1), 3–53.

Lenneberg, E. H. (1967). *Biological Foundations of Language*. New York: Wiley.

Leslie, A. M. & Frith, U. (1987). Metarepresentation and autism: How not to lose one's marbles. *Cognition, 27*(3), 291–294.

Levitin, D. J., Cole, K., Lincoln, A. & Bellugi, U. (2005). Aversion, awareness, and attraction: Investigating claims of hyperacusis in the Williams syndrome phenotype. *Journal of Child Psychology and Psychiatry, 46*(5), 514–523. doi: 10.1111/j.1469-7610.2004.00376.x.

Lewis, M. (1997). The self in self-conscious emotions. *Annals of the New York Academy of Sciences, 818*(1), 119–142.

Lewis, M. (2000). Self-conscious emotions. In M. Lewis & J. M. Haviland (Eds), *Handbook of Emotions*, 2nd edn (pp. 623–636). New York: Guilford.

Lewis, M. (2003). The role of the self in shame. *Social Research: An International Quarterly, 70*(4), 1181–1204.

Lewis, M. (2007). Self-conscious emotional development. In J. L. Tracy, R. W. Robins & J. P. Tangney (Eds), *The Self-conscious Emotions: Theory and Research* (pp. 134–149). New York: Guilford Press.

Lewis, M. & Michalson, L. (1983). *Children's Emotions and Moods: Developmental Theory and Measurement*. New York: Plenum Press.

Lewis, M., Stanger, C. & Sullivan, M. W. (1989). Deception in 3-year-olds. *Developmental Psychology*, *25*(3), 439–443. doi: 10.1037/0012-1649.25.3.439.

Lorenz, K. (1937). Imprinting. *Auk*, *54*(1), 245–273.

Lutz, D. J. & Sternberg, R. J. (1999). Cognitive development. In M. H. Bornstein & M. E. Lamb (Eds), *Developmental Pyschology*, 4th edn (pp. 275–311). New Jersey: Lawrence Erlbaum.

Mace, C., Moorey, S. & Roberts, B. (Eds) (2013). *Evidence in the Psychological Therapies: A Critical Guidance for Practitioners*. London: Routledge.

Main, M. (1990). Cross-cultural studies of attachment organization: Recent studies, changing methodologies, and the concept of conditional strategies. *Human Development*, *33*(1), 48–61.

Main, M. & Solomon, J. (1986). Discovery of an insecure-disorganized/disoriented attachment pattern. In T. B. Brazelton & M. W. Yogman (Eds), *Affective Development in Infancy* (pp. 95–124). Westport, CT: Ablex.

Malatesta, C. Z. & Haviland, J. M. (1982). Learning display rules: The socialization of emotion expression in infancy. *Child Development*, *53*, 991–1003.

Manassis, K. (2001). Child-parent relations: Attachment and anxiety disorders. New York: Cambridge University Press.

Marshall, W. L. (1989). Intimacy, loneliness and sexual offenders. *Behaviour Research and Therapy*, *27*(5), 491–504. doi: org/10.1016/0005-7967(89)90083-1.

Martin, G. B. & Clark, R. D. (1982). Distress crying in neonates: Species and peer specificity. *Developmental Psychology*, *18*(1), 3–9. doi: 10.1037/0012-1649.18.1.3.

Martin, C. L. & Fabes, R. A. (2008). *Discovering Child Development*. Boston, MA: Cengage Learning.

Masangkay, Z. S., McCluskey, K. A., McIntyre, C. W., Sims-Knight, J., Vaughn, B. E. & Flavell, J. H. (1974). The early development of inferences about the visual percepts of others. *Child Development*, *45*, 357–366.

McCambridge, J., Witton, J. & Elbourne, D. R. (2014). Systematic review of the Hawthorne effect: New concepts are needed to study research participation effects. *Journal of Clinical Epidemiology*, *67*(3), 267–277. doi: org/10.1016/j.jclinepi.2013.08.015.

McCrone, J. (1993). *The Myth of Irrationality: The Science of the Mind from Plato to Star Trek*. London: Macmillan.

McLeod, S. (2008). Erik Erikson. *Simply Psychology*. http://www.simplypsychology.org/Erik-Erikson.html.

Miller, P. H. (1993). *Theories of Developmental Psychology*. New York: Worth Publishers.

Millon, T. Millon, C. M., Meagher, S. Grossman, S. & Ramanath, R. (2004). *Personality Disorders in Modern Life*, 2nd edn. Hoboken, NJ: Wiley.

Minuchin. S. (1974). *Families and Family Therapy*. Cambridge, MA: Harvard University Press.

Minuchin, S., Lee, W. Y. & Simon, G. M. (2006). *Mastering Family Therapy: Journeys of Growth and Transformation*. New York: John Wiley.

Mireault, G. & Trahan, J. (2007). Tantrums and anxiety in early childhood: A pilot study. *Age*, *3*, 0–84.

Moon, C. Lagercrantz, H. & Kuhl, P. K. (2012). Language experienced *in utero* affects vowel perception after birth: A two-country study. *Acta Paediatrica*, *102*(2), 156–160. doi: 10.1111/apa.12098.

Morrison, A. P. (1989). *Shame: The Underside of Narcissism*. Hillsdale, NJ: Analytic Press.

Morrow, V. & Richards, M. (1996). The ethics of social research with children: An overview 1. *Children & Society*, *10*(2), 90–105. doi: 10.1111/j.1099-0860.1996.tb00461.x.

Moutsiana, C., Fearon, P., Murray, L., Cooper, P., Goodyer, I., Johnstone, T. & Halligan, S. (2014). Making an effort to feel positive: Insecure attachment in infancy predicts the neural underpinnings of emotion regulation in adulthood. *Journal of Child Psychology and Psychiatry*. doi: 10.1111/jcpp.12198.

Mueller, C. M. & Dweck, C. S. (1998). Praise for intelligence can undermine children's motivation and performance. *Journal of Personality & Social Psychology*, *75*, 33–35.

Newport, E. L. (1988). Constraints on learning and their role in language acquisition: Studies of the acquisition of American Sign Language. *Language Sciences*, *10*(1), 147–172. doi: org/10.1016/0388-0001(88)90010-1.

Nix, R. L., Bierman, K. L., Domitrovich, C. E. & Gill, S. (2013). Promoting children's social-emotional skills in preschool can enhance academic and behavioral functioning in kindergarten: Findings from head start REDI. *Early Education & Development*, *24*(7), 1000–1019. doi: 10.1080/10409289.2013.825565.

Noreika, V., Falter, C. M. & Rubia, K. (2013). Timing deficits in attention-deficit/hyperactivity disorder (ADHD): Evidence from neurocognitive and neuroimaging studies. *Neuropsychologia, 51*(2), 235–266. doi: 10.1016/j.neuropsychologia.2012.09.036.

Ornstein, A. C. (2012). *Foundations of Education.* Boston, MA: Cengage Learning.

Osterling, J. A., Dawson, G. & Munson, J. A. (2002). Early recognition of 1-year-old infants with autism spectrum disorder versus mental retardation. *Development and Psychopathology, 14*(2), 239–251. doi: /10.1017/S0954579402002031.

Pasalich, D. S., Dadds, M. R., Hawes, D. J. & Brennan, J. (2012). Attachment and callous-unemotional traits in children with early-onset conduct problems. *Journal of Child Psychology and Psychiatry, 53*(8), 838–845. doi: 10.1111/j.1469-7610.2012.02544.x.

Perner, J. (1991). *Understanding the Representational Mind.* Cambridge, MA: MIT Press.

Perner, J. & Wimmer, H. (1985). '*John thinks that Mary thinks that …*' attribution of second-order beliefs by 5- to 10-year-old children. *Journal of Experimental Child Psychology, 39*(3), 437–471. doi: org/10.1016/0022-0965(85)90051-7.

Perner, J., Leekam, S. R. & Wimmer, H. (1987). Three-year-olds' difficulty with false belief: The case for a conceptual deficit. *British Journal of Developmental Psychology, 5*(2), 125–137. doi: 10.1111/j.2044-835X.1987.tb01048.x.

Perry, B. D. (2002). Childhood experience and the expression of genetic potential: What childhood neglect tells us about nature and nurture. *Brain and Mind, 3*, 79–100. doi: 10.1023/A:1016557824657.

Peskin, J. (1992). Ruse and representations: On children's ability to conceal information. *Developmental Psychology, 28*(1), 84–89. doi: 10.1037/0012-1649.28.1.84.

Petersen, A. C. & Crockett, L. (1985). Pubertal timing and grade effects on adjustment. *Journal of Youth and Adolescence, 14*(3), 191–206.

Petersen, A. C. & Taylor, B. (1980). The biological approach to adolescence: Biological change and psychological adaptation. In J. Adelson (Ed.) *Handbook of Adolescent Psychology* (pp. 117–155). New York: Wiley.

Piaget, J. (1932). *The Moral Development of the Child.* London: Kegan Paul.

Piaget, J. (1952). *The Origins of Intelligence in Children*, transl. by M. T. Cook. New York: International Universities Press.

Piaget, J. (1954). *The Construction of Reality in the Child*. New York: Basic Books.

Piaget, J. ([1970] 1983). Piaget's theory. In P. H. Mussen (Series Ed.), *Handbook of Child Psychology: Vol. 1. History, Theory, and Methods*, 4th edn (pp. 103–128). New York: Wiley. [Original work published in 1970.]

Piaget, J. & Szeminska, A. (1941). *La genèse du nombre chez l'enfant*. Neuchâtel: Delachaux et Niestlé.

Pickles A. & Hill, J. W. (2006). Developmental pathways. In D. Cicchetti & D. J. Cohen (Eds), *Developmental Psychopathology: Vol. 1, Theory and Methods*, 2nd edn (pp. 211–243). Hoboken, NJ: Wiley.

Pinzon, J. L. & Jones, V. F. (2012). Care of adolescent parents and their children. *Pediatrics*, *130*(6), 1743–1756. doi: 10.1542/peds.2012-2879.

Plomin, R., DeFries, J. C., Knopik, V. S. & Neiderhiser, J. M. (2013). *Behavioral Genetics*, 6th edn. New York: Worth Publishers.

Premack, D. (1976). *Intelligence in Ape and Man*. Hillsdale, NJ: Lawrence Erlbaum.

Prior, V. & Glaser, D. (2006). *Understanding Attachment and Attachment Disorders: Theory, Evidence and Practice*. London: Jessica Kingsley Publishers.

Ramey, C. T. & Ramey, S. L. (1998). Early intervention and early experience. *American Psychologist*, *53*(2), 109–120.

Riggs, K. J., Peterson, D. M., Robinson, E. J. & Mitchell, P. (1998). Are errors in false belief tasks symptomatic of a broader difficulty with counterfactuality? *Cognitive Development*, *13*(1), 73–90. doi: org/10.1016/S0885-2014(98)90021-1.

Roberts, R. C. (2003). *Emotions: An Essay in Aid of Moral Psychology*. Cambridge: Cambridge University Press.

Rogoff, B. (1998). Cognition as a collaborative process. In W. Damon (Ed.) *Handbook of Child Psychology: Vol. 2, Cognition, Perception, and Language* (pp. 679–744). Hoboken, NJ: Wiley.

Rogol, A. D., Clark, P. A. & Roemmich, J. N. (2000). Growth and pubertal development in children and adolescents: Effects of diet and physical activity. *The American Journal of Clinical Nutrition*, *72*(2), 521s–528s.

Rogol, A. D., Roemmich, J. N. & Clark, P. A. (2002). Growth at puberty. *Journal of Adolescent Health*, *31*(6), 192–200. doi: org/10.1016/S1054-139X(02)00485-8.

Rothbart, M. K. & Bates, J. E. (2006). Temperament. In W. Damon, R. Leaner, & N. Eisenberg (Eds), *Handbook of Child Psychology: Vol. 3,*

Social, Emotional and Personality Development, 6th edn (pp. 99–166). New York: Wiley.

Rothbaum, F., Weisz, J., Pott, M., Miyake, K. & Morelli, G. (2000). Attachment and culture: Security in the United States and Japan. *American Psychologist*, *55*, 1093–1104. doi: 10.1037/0003-066X.55.10.1093.

Rousseau, J. J. ([1762] 1974). *Emile*, transl. by B. Foxley. London: Dent.

Rutter, M. (1990). Psychosocial resilience and protective mechanisms. In J. Rolf, A. S. Masten, D. Chichetti, K. H. Nuechterlin & S. Weintraub (Eds), *Risk and Protective Factors in the Development of Psychopathology* (pp. 181–214). New York: Cambridge University Press.

Rutter, M. (2000). Psychosocial influences: Critiques, findings, and research needs. *Development and Psychopathology*, *12*(3), 375-405.

Rutter, M. L. (2011). *Child Psychiatry: Modern Approaches*. Oxford: Blackwell.

Saarni, C. (1984). An observational study of children's attempts to monitor their expressive behavior. *Child Development*, *55*, 1504–1513.

Sagi, A., Van IJzendoorn, M. H. & Koren-Karie, N. (1991). Primary appraisal of the Strange Situation: A cross-cultural analysis of preseparation episodes. *Developmental Psychology*, *27*(4), 587–596. doi: 10.1037/0012-1649.27.4.587.

Savage-Rumbaugh, E. S. (1986). *Ape Language: From Conditioned Response to Symbol*. New York: Columbia University Press.

Saxe, R. (2006). Uniquely human social cognition. *Current Opinion in Neurobiology*, *16*(2), 235–239. doi: org/10.1016/j.conb.2006.03.001.

Schieffelin, B. & Ochs, E. (1987). *Language Acquisition across Cultures*. New York: Cambridge.

Schnack, H. G., van Haren, N. E., Brouwer, R. M., Evans, A., Durston, S., Boomsma, D. I. & Pol, H. E. H. (2014). Changes in thickness and surface area of the human cortex and their relationship with intelligence. *Cerebral Cortex*, advance access. doi: 10.1093/cercor/bht357.

Serbin, L. A., Moller, L. C, Gulko, J., Powlishta, K. K. & Colburne, K. A. (1994). The emergence of sex segregation in toddler playgroups. In C. Leaper (Ed.), *The Development of Gender and Relationships* (pp. 7–18). San Francisco: Jossey-Bas.

Shaffer, D. R., Wood, E. & Willoughby, T. (2002). Development of the self and social cognition. *Developmental Psychology: Childhood and Adolescence*, 5th edn (pp. 435–473), Scarborough, Canada: Thomson/Nelson.

Shatz, M., Wellman, H. M. & Silber, S. (1983). The acquisition of mental verbs: A systematic investigation of the first reference to mental state. *Cognition*, *14*(3), 301–321. doi: org/10.1016/0010-0277(83)90008-2.

Siegler, R. S. (1996). *Emerging Minds: The Process of Change in Children's Thinking*. Oxford & New York: Oxford University Press.

Silbereisen, R. K., Petersen, A. C., Albrecht, H. T. & Kracke, B. (1989). Maturational timing and the development of problem behavior longitudinal studies in adolescence. *The Journal of Early Adolescence*, *9*(3), 247–268. doi: 10.1177/0272431689093005.

Silventoinen, K., Bartels, M., Posthuma, D., Estourgie-van Burk, G. F., Willemsen, G., van Beijsterveldt, T. C. & Boomsma, D. I. (2007). Genetic regulation of growth in height and weight from 3 to 12 years of age: A longitudinal study of Dutch twin children. *Twin Research and Human Genetics*, *10*(02), 354–363. doi: org/10.1375/twin.10.2.354.

Skinner, B. F. (1957). *Verbal Behaviour*. New York: Appleton-Century Crofts.

Skinner, B. F. (1972). *Beyond Freedom and Dignity*. New York: Bantam Books.

Slavin, R. (2006). *Educational Psychology: Theory and Practice* 8th edn. Boston: Pearson.

Smallbone, S. W. & McCabe, B. A. (2003). Childhood attachment, childhood sexual abuse, and onset of masturbation among adult sexual offenders. *Sexual Abuse: A Journal of Research and Treatment*, *15*(1), 1–9. doi: 10.1023/A:1020616722684.

Smith, P. Cowie, H. & Blades, M. (2008). *Understanding Children's Development*. Chichester: Wiley.

Snow, C. E., Burns, M. S. & Griffin, P. (Eds) (1998). *Preventing Reading Difficulties in Young Children*. Washington, DC: National Academies Press.

Sorce, J. F., Emde, R. N., Campos, J. & Klinnert, M. D. (1985).Maternal emotional signaling: Its effects on the visual cliff behavior of 1-year-olds. *Developmental Psychology*, *21*(1), 195–200.

Sørensen, T. I., Holst, C. & Stunkard, A. J. (1992). Childhood body mass index: Genetic and familial environmental influences assessed in a longitudinal adoption study. *International Journal of Obesity and Related Metabolic Disorder*, *16*(9), 705–714.

Spelke, E. S. (1991). Physical knowledge in infancy: Reflections on Piaget's theory. In S. Carey & R. Gelman (Eds), *The Epigenesis of Mind: Essays on Biology and Cognition* (pp. 133–169). Hillsdale, NJ: Lawrence Erlbaum.

Sroufe, L. A. (2005). Attachment and development: A prospective, longitudinal study from birth to adulthood. *Attachment & Human Development*, *7*(4), 349–367.

Steele, M., Hodges, J., Kaniuk, J., Hillman, S. & Henderson, K. (2003). Attachment representations and adoption: Associations between maternal states of mind and emotion narratives in previously maltreated children. *Journal of Child Psychotherapy*, *29*(2), 187–205. doi: 10.1080/0075417031000138442.

Stevenson-Hinde, J. & Shouldice, A. (2013). Wariness to strangers: A behavior systems perspective. In K. H. Rubin & J. Asendorpf (Eds), *Social Withdrawal, Inhibition, and Shyness in Childhood* (pp. 101–116). New York: Psychology Press.

Stevenson-Snell, H. (1996). Psychometric testing: Clinical, behavioural and psychodynamic uses of two psychometric tests-BHS and RISC. *Employee Counselling Today*, *8*(1), 9–18.

Swettenham, J., Baron-Cohen, S., Charman, T., Cox, A., Baird, G., Drew, A. & Wheelwright, S. (1998). The frequency and distribution of spontaneous attention shifts between social and nonsocial stimuli in autistic, typically developing, and nonautistic developmentally delayed infants. *Journal of Child Psychology and Psychiatry*, *39*(5), 747–753. doi: 10.1111/1469-7610.0037.

Tager-Flusberg, H. (1999). A psychological approach to understanding the social and language impairments in autism. *International Review of Psychiatry*, *11*(4), 325–334. doi: 10.1080/09540269974203.

Tangney, J. P., Stuewig, J. & Mashek, D. J. (2007). What's moral about the self-conscious emotions. In J. L. Tracy, R. W. Robins & J. P. Tangney (Eds), *The Self-Conscious Emotions: Theory and Research* (pp. 21–37). New York: Guilford Press.

Tangney, J. P., Stuewig, J., Mashek, D. & Hastings, M. (2011). Assessing jail inmates' proneness to shame and guilt: Feeling bad about the behavior or the self? *Criminal Justice and Behavior*, *38*(7), 710–734. doi: 10.1177/0093854811405762.

Taumoepeau, M. & Reese, E. (2013). Understanding the self through siblings: Self-awareness mediates the sibling effect on social understanding. *Social Development*, *23*(1), 1–18. doi: 10.1111/sode.12035.

Thiessen, E. D., Hill, E. A. & Saffran, J. R. (2005). Infant-directed speech facilitates word segmentation. *Infancy*, *7*(1), 53–71. doi: 10.1207/s15327078in0701_5.

Tomasello, M. (1993). Joint attention as social cognition. In C. Moore & P. J. Dunham (Eds), *Joint Attention: Its Origins and Role in Development* (pp. 103–130). Hillsdale, NJ: Lawrence Erlbaum.

Tucker, C. J., Updegraff, K. A., McHale, S. M. & Crouter, A. C. (1999). Older siblings as socializers of younger siblings' empathy. *The Journal of Early Adolescence*, *19*(2), 176–198. doi: 10.1177/0272431699019002003.

Turiel, E. (1983). Domains and categories in social-cognitive development. In W. Overton (Ed.), *The Relationship Between Social and Cognitive Development* (pp. 53–89). Hillsdale, NJ: Erlbaum.

Uccelli, P., Barr, C. D., Dobbs, C. L., Galloway, E. P., Meneses, A. & Sanchez, E. (2014). Core Academic Language Skills (CALS): An expanded operational construct and a novel instrument to chart school-relevant language proficiency in per-adolescent and adolescent learner. *Applied Psycholinguistics*, forthcoming.

Uher, R. (2014). Gene–environment interactions in common mental disorders: An update and strategy for a genome-wide search. *Social Psychiatry and Psychiatric Epidemiology*, *49*(1), 3–14. doi: 10.1007/s00127-013-0801-0.

Vaish, A. & Striano, T. (2004). Is visual reference necessary? Contributions of facial versus vocal cues in 12-month-olds' social referencing behavior. *Developmental Science*, *7*(3), 261–269. doi: 10.1111/j.1467-7687.2004.00344.x.

Van IJzendoorn, M. H. & Kroonenberg, P. M. (1988). Cross-cultural patterns of attachment: A meta-analysis of the Strange Situation. *Child Development*, *59*(1), 147–156.

Verhoof, E., Maurice-Stam, H., Heymans, H. & Grootenhuis, M. (2013). Health-related quality of life, anxiety and depression in young adults with disability benefits due to childhood-onset somatic conditions. *Child and Adolescent Psychiatry and Mental Health*, *7*(1), 12. doi: 10.1186/1753-2000-7-12.

Vigil, D. C., Hodges, J. & Klee, T. (2005). Quantity and quality of parental language input to late-talking toddlers during play. *Child Language Teaching and Therapy*, *21*(2), 107–122. doi: 10.1191/0265659005ct284oa.

Visscher, P. M., Medland, S. E., Ferreira, M. A. R., Morley, K. I., Zhu, G., Cornes, B. K., Montgomery, G. W. & Martin, N. G (2006). Assumption-free estimation of heritability from genome-wide identity-by-descent sharing between full siblings. *PLoS Genetics*, *2*(3), e41. doi: 10.1371/journal.pgen.0020041.

Vygotsky, L. S. (1978). *Mind in Society: The Development of Higher Psychological Processes*. Cambridge, MA: Harvard University Press.

Vygotsky, L. S. (1984). Problema vozrasta [The problem of age]. In *L. S. Vygotsky, Sobranie socinenij* [Collected works] (Vol. IV). Moscow: Pedagogika.

Vygotsky, L. S. (1986). Konkretnaya psikhologiya cheloveka [A concrete psychology of man]. *Vestnik Moskovskogo Universiteta. Seriya 14. Psikhologiya* (pp. 52–65). [In Russian.]

Vygotsky, L. S. (1987). *The Collected Works of L.S. Vygotsky: Problems of General Psychology*, edited by R. W. Rieber & A. S. Carton, transl. by N. Minwick. New York: Plenum.

Wardhaugh, R. (1993). *Investigating Language, Central Problems in Linguistics*. Oxford & Cambridge, MA: Blackwell.

Waters, E., Petters, D. & Facompre, C. (2013). Epilogue: Reflections on a Special Issue of Attachment & Human Development in Mary Ainsworth's 100th year. *Attachment & Human Development*, *15*(5–6), 673–681.

Watson, J. B. (1913). Psychology as the behaviorist sees it. *Psychology Review*, *20*, 158–177.

Weir, R. H. (1962). *Language in the Crib*. Janua Linguarum 14. The Hague: Mouton.

Wellman, H. M. & Estes, D. (1986). Early understanding of mental entities: A reexamination of childhood realism. *Child Development*, 57(4), 910–923.

Wertsch, J. V. (1991). *Voices of the Mind: Sociocultural Approach to Mediated Action*. Cambridge, MA: Harvard University Press.

Weston, D. R. & Turiel, E. (1980). Act–rule relations: Children's concepts of social rules. *Developmental Psychology*, *16*(5), 417–424. doi: 10.1037/0012-1649.16.5.417.

Wichstrøm, L. (1999). The emergence of gender difference in depressed mood during adolescence: The role of intensified gender socialization. *Developmental Psychology*, *35*(1), 232–245. doi: 10.1037/0012-1649.35.1.232.

Williams, J. M. & Dunlop, L. C. (1999). Pubertal timing and self-reported delinquency among male adolescents. *Journal of Adolescence*, *22*(1), 157–171. doi: org/10.1006/jado.1998.0208.

Wimmer, H. & Perner, J. (1983). Beliefs about beliefs: Representation and constraining function of wrong beliefs in young children's understanding of deception. *Cognition*, *13*(1), 103–128. doi: org/10.1016/0010-0277(83)90004-5.

Wing, L. (1991). The relationship between Asperger's syndrome and Kanner's autism. In U. Frith (Ed.) *Autism and Asperger Syndrome* (pp. 93–121). Cambridge: Cambridge University Press.

Wood, D., Bruner, J. S. & Ross, G. (1976). The role of tutoring in problem solving. *Journal of Child Psychology and Psychiatry*, *17*(2), 89–100. doi: 10.1111/j.1469-7610.1976.tb00381.x.

Wortman, C., Loftus, E. & Weaver, C. (1999). *Psychology*, 5th edn. New York: Harper Collins College.

Youngblade, L. M. & Dunn, J. (1995). Individual differences in young children's pretend play with mother and sibling: Links to relationships and understanding of other people's feelings and beliefs. *Child Development*, *66*(5), 1472–1492. doi: 1111/j.1467-8624.1995.tb00946.x.

Zahn-Waxler, C., Radke-Yarrow, M., Wagner, E. & Chapman, M. (1992). Development of concern for others. *Developmental Psychology*, *28*(1), 126–136. doi: 10.1037/0012-1649.28.1.126.

Zhou, Q., Eisenberg, N., Losoya, S. H., Fabes, R. A., Reiser, M., Guthrie, I. K., Murphy, B. C., Cumberland, A. J. & Shepard, S. A. (2002). The relations of parental warmth and positive expressiveness to children's empathy-related responding and social functioning: A longitudinal study. *Child Development*, *73*(3), 893–915. doi: 10.1111/1467-8624.00446.

Index